teach
yourself

linguistics

teach yourself®

linguistics
jean aitchison

For over 60 years, more than 50 million people have learnt over 750 subjects the **teach yourself** way, with impressive results.

be where you want to be
with **teach yourself**

The publisher has used its best endeavours to ensure that the URLs for external websites referred to in this book are correct and active at the time of going to press. However, the publisher and the author have no responsibility for the websites and can make no guarantee that a site will remain live or that the content will remain relevant, decent or appropriate.

First printed under the title *General Linguistics* 1972 Second edition 1978 Third edition 1987 Fourth edition 1992 Fifth edition 1999 Sixth edition 2003

For UK order enquiries: please contact Bookpoint Ltd, 130 Milton Park, Abingdon, Oxon, OX14 4SB. Telephone: +44 (0) 1235 827720. Fax: +44 (0) 1235 400454. Lines are open 09.00–17.00, Monday to Saturday, with a 24-hour message answering service. Details about our titles and how to order are available at www.teachyourself.co.uk

For USA order enquiries: please contact McGraw-Hill Customer Services, PO Box 545, Blacklick, OH 43004-0545, USA. Telephone: 1-800-722-4726. Fax: 1-614-755-5645.

For Canada order enquiries: please contact McGraw-Hill Ryerson Ltd, 300 Water St, Whitby, Ontario, L1N 9B6, Canada. Telephone: 905 430 5000. Fax: 905 430 5020.

Long renowned as the authoritative source for self-guided learning – with more than 50 million copies sold worldwide – the **teach yourself** series includes over 500 titles in the fields of languages, crafts, hobbies, business, computing and education.

British Library Cataloguing in Publication Data: a catalogue record for this title is available from the British Library.

Library of Congress Catalog Card Number: on file.

First published in UK 1999 by Hodder Education, 338 Euston Road, London, NW1 3BH.

First published in US 1999 by The McGraw-Hill Companies, Inc.

This edition published 2003.

The **teach yourself** name is a registered trade mark of Hodder Headline.

Copyright © 1999, 2003 Jean Aitchison

In UK: All rights reserved. Apart from any permitted use under UK copyright law, no part of this publication may be reproduced or transmitted in any form or by any means, electronic or mechanical, including photocopy, recording, or any information, storage and retrieval system, without permission in writing from the publisher or under licence from the Copyright Licensing Agency Limited. Further details of such licences (for reprographic reproduction) may be obtained from the Copyright Licensing Agency Limited, of Saffron House, 6–10 Kirby Street, London, EC1N 8TS.

In US: All rights reserved. Except as permitted under the United States Copyright Act of 1976, no part of this publication may be reproduced or distributed in any form or by any means, or stored in a database or retrieval system, without the prior written permission of the publisher.

Typeset by Transet Limited, Coventry, England.
Printed in Great Britain for Hodder Education, a division of Hodder Headline, an Hachette Livre UK Company, 338 Euston Road, London, NW1 3BH, by Cox & Wyman Ltd, Reading, Berkshire.

Hodder Headline's policy is to use papers that are natural, renewable and recyclable products and made from wood grown in sustainable forests. The logging and manufacturing processes are expected to conform to the environmental regulations of the country of origin.

Impression number   12 11 10 9
Year   2010 2009 2008 2007

contents

vi contents

preface

This book is an introduction to introductions to linguistics.

There are several books on the market which call themselves 'introductions' to the subject, but which are in fact more suited to second-year students.

This book is to help people working by themselves to break into the 'charmed circle' of linguistics. It explains basic concepts and essential terminology.

It is not a bedside reading book, and contains no chatty anecdotes. It is a straightforward handbook for those who wish to know about the subject. Linguistics is a highly technical field, and technical vocabulary cannot be avoided.

Linguistics is a field torn apart by controversies. Wherever possible, I have taken a 'middle-of-the-road' view. Not that a middle-of-the-road view is necessarily right, but it is possibly more helpful for those new to the subject. Hopefully, readers will view this book as a stepping-stone to some of the works suggested for further reading (p. 231), and will eventually decide for themselves on which side of the road they wish to stand over current linguistics issues.

Linguistics is a fast-changing subject, and parts of it have moved on considerably since the first edition of this book was published (1972). Above all, linguistics has continued to expand, like a tree which grows numerous new branches. This new edition contains a number of changes, including a revised and extended list of suggestions for further reading.

I am most grateful to all those who have made helpful suggestions and comments, especially to any students or readers who spotted errors in the older editions. I hope none remain in this new edition, but if anyone finds any, I would be very grateful to know about them. Warm thanks go also to Diana Lewis of the University of Oxford, who did such a careful revision of the index.

In this edition, as in the previous one, I have tried to avoid sexist language. I have done this partly by using the plural (*people* instead of *he*), partly by using indefinites (*a person, anyone*) followed by a plural pronoun (*if anyone is surprised, they should see how increasingly common this usage is*), and partly by interchanging *he* and *she* in places where a neutral between sexes pronoun is required.

Acknowledgements

The author and publishers thank the following for permission to reproduce material in this book: The Estate of the late Sir Alan Herbert for a passage from *What a Word* by A. P. Herbert, and to Dr J. B. Searle for his limerick 'There was a young man of Dunlaoghaire'.

André Deutsch Ltd/Little Brown/Curtis Brown Ltd for two lines from the poem 'The Octopus' by Ogden Nash.

The Society of Authors as the Literary Representative of the Estate of John Masefield for two lines from the poem 'Cargoes'.

'Politics and the English Language' by George Orwell copyright © George Orwell, 1946 by permission of A. M. Heath on behalf of Martin Secker & Warburg Ltd and Mark Hamilton as the Literary Executor of the Late Sonia Brownell Orwell.

The Society of Authors as the Literary Representative of the estate of A. E. Housman for the extract from 'A Shropshire Lad' from *The Collective Poems of A. E. Housman*.

David Higham Associates and New Directions for the extract from Dylan Thomas's 'A Child's Christmas in Wales'.

Random House UK Ltd for the extract from D. J. Enright's *A Mania for Sentences*.

Faber & Faber Ltd and Harcourt, Brace & Company for the extract from T. S. Eliot's 'Little Gidding' from *The Four Quartets*.

Every effort has been made to contact the holders of copyright material but if any have been inadvertently overlooked, the publisher will be pleased to make the necessary alterations at the first opportunity.

part one

starting out

Worry about words, Bobby. Your grandmother is right. For, whatever else you may do, you will be using words always. All day, and every day, words matter. Though you live in a barrel and speak to nobody but yourself, words matter. For words are the tools of thought …

A.P. Herbert

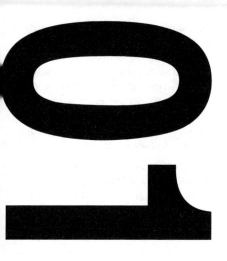

01

what is linguistics?

This chapter explains how
linguistics differs from
traditional grammar studies,
and outlines the main
subdivisions of the subject.

Most people spend an immense amount of their life talking, listening, and, in advanced societies, reading and writing, Normal conversation uses 4,000 to 5,000 words an hour. A radio talk, where there are fewer pauses, uses as many as 8,000 to 9,000 words per hour. A person reading at a normal speed covers 14,000 to 15,000 words per hour. So someone who chats for an hour, listens to a radio talk for an hour and reads for an hour possibly comes into contact with 25,000 words in that time. Per day, the total could be as high as 100,000.

The use of language is an integral part of being human. Children all over the world start putting words together at approximately the same age, and follow remarkably similar paths in their speech development. All languages are surprisingly similar in their basic structure, whether they are found in South America, Australia or near the North Pole. Language and abstract thought are closely connected, and many people think that these two characteristics above all distinguish human beings from animals.

An inability to use language adequately can affect someone's status in society, and may even alter their personality. Because of its crucial importance in human life, every year an increasing number of psychologists, sociologists, anthropologists, teachers, speech therapists, computer scientists and copywriters (to name but a few professional groups) realize that they need to study language more deeply. So it is not surprising that in recent years one of the fastest-expanding branches of knowledge has been linguistics – the systematic study of language.

Linguistics tries to answer the basic questions 'What is language?' and 'How does language work?'. It probes into various aspects of these problems, such as 'What do all languages have in common?', 'What range of variation is found among languages?', 'How does human language differ from animal communication?', 'How does a child learn to speak?', 'How does one write down and analyze an unwritten language?', 'Why do languages change?', 'To what extent are social class differences reflected in language?' and so on.

What is a linguist?

A person who studies linguistics is usually referred to as a **linguist**. The more accurate term 'linguistician' is too much of a tongue-twister to become generally accepted. The word 'linguist' is unsatisfactory: it causes confusion, since it also refers to someone who speaks a large number of languages. Linguists in the sense of linguistics experts need not be fluent in languages, though they must have a wide experience of different types of languages. It is more important for them to analyze and explain linguistic phenomena such as the Turkish vowel system, or German verbs, than to make themselves understood in Istanbul or Berlin. They are skilled, objective observers rather than participants – consumers of languages rather than producers, as one social scientist flippantly commented.

Our type of linguist is perhaps best likened to a musicologist. A musicologist could analyze a piano concerto by pointing out the theme and variations, harmony and counterpoint. But such a person need not actually play the concerto, a task left to the concert pianist. Music theory bears the same relation to actual music as linguistics does to language.

How does linguistics differ from traditional grammar?

One frequently meets people who think that linguistics is old school grammar jazzed up with a few new names. But it differs in several basic ways.

First, and most important, linguistics is **descriptive**, not prescriptive. Linguists are interested in what *is* said, not what they think *ought* to be said. They describe language in all its aspects, but do not prescribe rules of 'correctness'.

It is a common fallacy that there is some absolute standard of correctness which it is the duty of linguists, schoolmasters, grammars and dictionaries to maintain. There was an uproar in America when in 1961 *Webster's Third New International Dictionary of the English Language* included words such as *ain't* and phrases such as *ants in one's pants*. The editors were deliberately corrupting the language – or else they were incompetent, argued the critics. 'Webster III has thrust upon us a dismaying assortment of the questionable, the perverse, the unworthy and the downright outrageous', said one angry reviewer. But if people say *ain't* and *ants in one's pants*, linguists consider it important to record the fact. They are observers and recorders, not judges.

'I am irritated by the frequent use of the words *different to* on radio and other programmes' ran a letter to a daily paper. 'In my schooldays of fifty years ago we were taught that things were *alike to* and *different from.* Were our teachers so terribly ignorant?' This correspondent has not realized that languages are constantly changing. And the fact that he comments on the *frequent* use of *different to* indicates that it has as much right to be classified as 'correct' as *different from.*

The notion of absolute and unchanging 'correctness' is quite foreign to linguists. They might recognize that one type of speech appears, through the whim of fashion, to be more socially acceptable than others. But this does not make the socially acceptable variety any more interesting for them than the other varieties, or the old words any better than new ones. To linguists the language of a pop singer is not intrinsically worse (or better) than that of a duke. They would disagree strongly with the *Daily Telegraph* writer who complained that 'a disc jockey talking to the latest Neanderthal pop idol is a truly shocking experience of verbal squalor'. Nor do linguists condemn the coining of new words. This is a natural and continuous process, not a sign of decadence and decay. A linguist would note with interest, rather than horror, the fact that you can have your hair washed and set in a *glamorama* in North Carolina, or your car oiled at a *lubritorium* in Sydney, or that you can buy apples at a *fruitique* in a trendy suburb of London.

A second important way in which linguistics differs from traditional school grammar is that linguists regard the **spoken** language as primary, not the written. In the past, grammarians have over-stressed the importance of the written word, partly because of its permanence. It was difficult to cope with fleeting utterances before the invention of sound recording. The traditional classical education was also partly to blame. People insisted on moulding language in accordance with the usage of the 'best authors' of classical times, and these authors existed only in written form. This attitude began as far back as the 2nd century BC when scholars in Alexandria took the authors of 5th-century Greece as their models. This belief in the superiority of the written word has continued for over two millennia.

But linguists look first at the spoken word, which preceded the written everywhere in the world, as far as we know. Moreover, most writing systems are derived from the vocal sounds. Although spoken utterances and written sentences share many common features, they also exhibit considerable differences.

Linguists therefore regard spoken and written forms as belonging to different, though overlapping systems, which must be analyzed separately: the spoken first, then the written.

A third way in which linguistics differs from traditional grammar studies is that it does not force languages into a Latin-based framework. In the past, many traditional textbooks have assumed unquestioningly that Latin provides a universal framework into which all languages fit, and countless schoolchildren have been confused by meaningless attempts to force English into foreign patterns. It is sometimes claimed, for example, that a phrase such as *for John* is in the 'dative case'. But this is blatantly untrue, since English does not have a Latin-type case system. At other times, the influence of the Latin framework is more subtle, and so more misleading. Many people have wrongly come to regard certain Latin categories as being 'natural' ones. For example, it is commonly assumed that the Latin tense divisions of past, present and future are inevitable. Yet one frequently meets languages which do not make this neat threefold distinction. In some languages, it is more important to express the duration of an action – whether it is a single act or a continuing process – than to locate the action in time.

In addition, judgements on certain constructions often turn out to have a Latin origin. For example, people frequently argue that 'good English' avoids 'split infinitives' as in the phrase *to humbly apologize*, where the infinitive *to apologize* is 'split' by *humbly*. A letter to the London *Evening Standard* is typical of many: 'Do split infinitives madden your readers as much as they do me?' asks the correspondent. 'Can I perhaps ask that, at least, judges and editors make an effort to maintain the form of our language?' The idea that a split infinitive is wrong is based on Latin. Purists insist that, because a Latin infinitive is only one word, its English equivalent must be as near to one word as possible. To linguists, it is unthinkable to judge one language by the standards of another. Since split infinitives occur frequently in English, they are as 'correct' as unsplit ones.

In brief, linguists are opposed to the notion that any one language can provide an adequate framework for all the others. They are trying to set up a universal framework. And there is no reason why this should resemble the grammar of Latin, or the grammar of any other language arbitrarily selected from the thousands spoken by humans.

The scope of linguistics

Linguistics covers a wide range of topics and its boundaries are difficult to define.

A diagram in the shape of a wheel gives a rough impression of the range covered (Figure 1.1).

In the centre is **phonetics**, the study of human speech sounds. A good knowledge of phonetics is useful for a linguist. Yet it is a basic background knowledge, rather than part of linguistics itself. Phoneticians are concerned with the actual physical sounds, the raw material out of which language is made. They study the position of the tongue, teeth and vocal cords during the production of sounds, and record and analyze sound waves. Linguists, on the other hand, are more interested in the way in which language is patterned. They analyze the shape or **form** of these patterns rather than the physical substance out of which the units of language are made. The famous Swiss linguist,

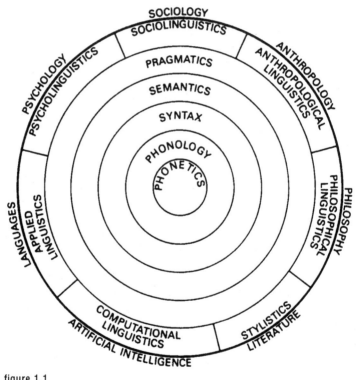

figure 1.1

Ferdinand de Saussure, expressed the difference well when he compared language with a game of chess. The linguist is interested in the various moves which the chessmen make and how they are aligned on the board. It does not matter whether the chessmen are made of wood or ivory. Their substance does not alter the rules of the game.

Although phonetics and linguistics are sometimes referred to together as 'the linguistic sciences', phonetics is not as central to general linguistics as the study of language patterning. For this reason, information about phonetics has been placed in an appendix at the end of the book.

In Figure 1.1, phonetics is surrounded by **phonology** (sound patterning), then phonology is surrounded by **syntax**. The term 'syntax', used in its broadest sense, refers to both the arrangement and the form of words. It is that part of language which links together the sound patterns and the meaning. **Semantics** (meaning) is placed outside syntax. Phonology, syntax and semantics are the 'bread and butter' of linguistics, and are a central concern of this book. Together they constitute the **grammar** of a language (Figure 1.2).

GRAMMAR

figure 1.2

But a word of warning about differences in terminology must be added. In some (usually older) textbooks, the word 'grammar' has a more restricted use. It refers only to what we have called the syntax. In these books, the term 'syntax' is restricted to the arrangement of words, and the standard term **morphology** is used for their make-up. This is not a case of one group of linguists being right in their use of terminology, and the other wrong, but of words gradually shifting their meaning, with the terms 'syntax' and 'grammar' extending their range.

Around the central grammatical hub comes **pragmatics**, which deals with how speakers use language in ways which cannot be predicted from linguistic knowledge alone. This relatively new and fast expanding topic has connections both with semantics, and with the various branches of linguistics which link language with the external world: **psycholinguistics** (the study of language and mind), **sociolinguistics** (the study of language and society), **applied linguistics** (the application of linguistics to language teaching), **computational linguistics** (the use of computers to simulate language and its workings), **stylistics** (the study of language and literature), **anthropological linguistics** (the study of language in cross-cultural settings), **philosophical linguistics** (the link between language and logical thought).

These various branches overlap to some extent, so are hard to define clearly. Psycholinguistics, sociolinguistics and stylistics are perhaps the ones which have expanded fastest in recent years. For this reason, they are given chapters to themselves in this book.

Finally, there are two important aspects of linguistics which have been omitted from the diagram. The first is **historical linguistics**, the study of language change. This omission was inevitable in a two-dimensional diagram. But if the wheel diagram is regarded as three-dimensional, as if it were the cross-section of a tree, then we can include this topic. We can either look at a grammar at one particular point in time (a single cut across the tree), or we can study its development over a number of years, by comparing a number of different cuts made across the tree trunk at different places (Figure 1.3).

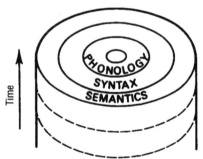

figure 1.3

Because it is normally necessary to know how a system works at any one time before one can hope to understand changes, the analysis of language at a single point in time, or **synchronic** linguistics, is usually dealt with before historical or **diachronic** linguistics.

The second omission is **linguistic typology,** the study of different language types. This could not be fitted in because it spreads over several layers of the diagram, covering phonology, syntax and semantics.

This chapter has explained how linguistics differs from traditional grammar studies, and has outlined the main subdivisions within the subject. The next chapter will look at the phenomenon studied by linguistics, **language.**

Questions

Test yourself on what you have read in Chapter 1 by answering the following questions.

1 How would you define **linguistics**?
2 Point out three ways in which linguistics differs from traditional school grammar.
3 What is the difference between a **prescriptive** and a **descriptive** approach to language?
4 Why do linguists regard speech rather than writing as primary?
5 Briefly explain the terms **phonology**, **syntax** and **semantics**.
6 Distinguish between **synchronic** and **diachronic** linguistics.

02

what is language?

This chapter outlines some important 'design features' of human language, and explores the extent to which they are found in animal communication. It also looks at the main purposes for which language is used.

Linguistics can be defined as 'the systematic study of language' – a discipline which describes language in all its aspects and formulates theories as to how it works.

But what exactly *is* language? People often use the word in a very wide sense: 'the language of flowers', 'the language of music', 'body language' and so on. This book, in common with most linguistics books, uses the word to mean the specialized sound signalling system which seems to be genetically programmed to develop in humans. Humans can, of course, communicate in numerous other ways: they can wink, wave, smile, tap someone on the shoulder, and so on. This wider study is usually known as 'the psychology of communication'. It overlaps with linguistics, but is not the concern of this book.

It is also clear that humans can transfer language to various other media: written symbols, braille, sign language, and so on. Sign language in particular has interesting characteristics which are not all predictable from the spoken word. However, language based on sound is more widespread, and perhaps more basic, and so has been given priority in this book.

But can language be defined? And how can it be distinguished from other systems of animal communication? A useful approach was pioneered by the American linguist Charles Hockett. This is to make a list of **design features**, and to consider whether they are shared by other animals. Some important ones will be discussed in the next few pages.

Use of sound signals

When animals communicate with one another, they may do so by a variety of means. Crabs, for example, communicate by waving their claws at one another, and bees have a complicated series of 'dances' which signify the whereabouts of a source of nectar.

But such methods are not as widespread as the use of sounds, which are employed by humans, grasshoppers, birds, dolphins, cows, monkeys, and many other species. So our use of sound is in no way unique. Sound signals have several advantages. They can be used in the dark, and at some distance, they allow a wide variety of messages to be sent, and they leave the body free for other activities.

Humans probably acquired their sound signalling system at a fairly late stage in their evolution. This seems likely because all the organs used in speech have some more basic function. The lungs are primarily used for breathing. Teeth, lips and tongue are primarily for eating. The vocal cords (thin strips of membrane deep in the throat) were used primarily for closing off the lungs in order to make the rib cage rigid for actions requiring a great effort. When people lift something heavy, they automatically hold their breath. This is caused by the closing of the vocal cords. The grunt when the heavy object is dropped is caused by the air being expelled as the vocal cords open. Millions of years ago we possibly needed a rigid rib cage for swinging in the trees – but humans still need this mechanism today for such actions as weightlifting, defecation and childbirth.

Arbitrariness

There is often a strong recognizable link between the actual signal and the message an animal wishes to convey. An animal who wishes to warn off an opponent may simulate an attacking attitude. A cat, for example, will arch its back, spit and appear ready to pounce.

In human language, the reverse is true. In the great majority of cases, there is no link whatsoever between the signal and the message. The symbols used are **arbitrary**. There is no intrinsic connection, for example, between the word *elephant* and the animal it symbolizes. Nor is the phrase 'These bananas are bad' intrinsically connected with food. Onomatopoeic words such as *quack-quack* and *bang* are exceptions – but there are relatively few of these compared with the total number of words.

The need for learning

Many animals automatically know how to communicate without learning. Their systems of communication are genetically inbuilt. Bee-dancing, for example, is substantially the same in bee colonies in different parts of the world, with only small variations. Even in cases where an element of learning is involved, this is usually minor. In one experiment a chaffinch reared in a soundproof room away from other chaffinches developed an abnormal type of song. Yet when the bird was exposed to only occasional tape recordings of other chaffinches, its song developed normally.

This is quite different from the long learning process needed to acquire human language, which is culturally transmitted. A human being brought up in isolation simply does not acquire language, as is shown by the rare studies of children brought up by animals without human contact. Human language is by no means totally conditioned by the environment, and there is almost certainly some type of innate predisposition towards language in a new-born child. But this latent potentiality can be activated only by long exposure to language, which requires careful learning.

Duality

Animals who use vocal signals have a stock of basic sounds which vary according to species. A cow has under ten, a chicken has around twenty, and a fox over thirty. Dolphins have between twenty and thirty, and so do gorillas and chimpanzees. Most animals can use each basic sound only once. That is, the number of messages an animal can send is restricted to the number of basic sounds, or occasionally the basic sounds plus a few simple combinations.

Human language works rather differently. Each language has a stock of sound units or **phonemes** which are similar in number to the basic sounds possessed by animals; the average number is between thirty and forty. But each phoneme is normally meaningless in isolation. It becomes meaningful only when it is combined with other phonemes. That is, sounds such as *f, g, d, o,* mean nothing separately. They normally take on meaning only when they are combined together in various ways, as in *fog, dog, god.*

This organization of language into two layers – a layer of sounds which combine into a second layer of larger units – is known as **duality** or **double articulation**. A communication system with duality is considerably more flexible than one without it, because a far greater number of messages can be sent.

At one time, it was thought that duality was a characteristic unique to human language. But now some people claim that it exists also in birdsong, where each individual note is meaningless. It is the combination of notes into longer sequences which constitutes a meaningful melody.

Displacement

Most animals can communicate about things in the immediate environment only. A bird utters its danger cry only when danger is present. It cannot give information about a peril which is removed in time and place. This type of spontaneous utterance is nearer to a human baby's emotional cries of pain, hunger or contentment than it is to fully developed language.

Human language, by contrast, can communicate about things that are absent as easily as about things that are present. This apparently rare phenomenon, known as **displacement**, does occasionally occur in the animal world, for example, in the communication of honey bees. If a worker bee finds a new source of nectar, it returns to the hive and performs a complex dance in order to inform the other bees of the exact location of the nectar, which may be several miles away. But even bees are limited in this ability. They can inform each other only about nectar. Human language can cope with any subject whatever, and it does not matter how far away the topic of conversation is in time and space.

Creativity (Productivity)

Most animals have a very limited number of messages they can send or receive. The male of a certain species of grasshopper, for example, has a choice of six, which might be translated as follows:

1 I am happy, life is good.
2 I would like to make love.
3 You are trespassing on my territory.
4 She's mine.
5 Let's make love.
6 Oh how nice to have made love.

Not only is the number of messages fixed for the grasshopper, but so are the circumstances under which each can be communicated. All animals, as far as we know, are limited in a similar way. Bees can communicate only about nectar. Dolphins, in spite of their intelligence and large number of clicks, whistles and squawks, seem to be restricted to communicating about the same things again and again. And even the clever vervet monkey, who is claimed to make thirty-six different vocal sounds, is obliged to repeat these over and over.

This type of restriction is not found in human language, which is essentially **creative** (or **productive**). Humans can produce novel utterances whenever they want to. A person can utter a sentence which has never been said before, in the most unlikely circumstances, and still be understood. If, at a party, someone said, 'There is a purple platypus crawling across the ceiling', friends might think the speaker was drunk or drugged, but they would still understand the words spoken. Conversely, in an everyday routine situation, a person is not obliged to say the same thing every time. At breakfast, someone might say 'This is good coffee' on one day, 'Is this coffee or dandelion tea?' on the next, and 'It would be cheaper to drink petrol' on the next.

Patterning

Many animal communication systems consist of a simple list of elements. There is no internal organization within the system.

Human language, on the other hand, is most definitely not a haphazard heap of individual items. Humans do not juxtapose sounds and words in a random way. Instead, they ring the changes on a few well-defined patterns.

Take the sounds *a*, *b*, *s*, *t*. In English, there are only four possible ways in which these sounds could be arranged, *bats*, *tabs*, *stab* or *bast* (the latter meaning 'inner bark of lime', *Oxford English Dictionary*). All other possibilities, such as **sbat*, **abts*, **stba*, are excluded (an asterisk indicates an impossible word or sentence). The starred words are not excluded in this case because such sequences are unpronounceable, but because the 'rules' subconsciously followed by people who know English do not allow these combinations, even for new words. A new washing powder called *Sbat* would be unlikely to catch on, since English does not permit the initial sequence *sb*, even though in some other languages (for example, ancient Greek) this combination is not unusual.

Similarly, consider the words, *burglar, loudly, sneezed, the*. Here again, only three combinations are possible: *The burglar sneezed loudly, Loudly sneezed the burglar* and (perhaps) *The burglar loudly sneezed*. All others are impossible, such as **The loudly burglar sneezed*, or **Sneezed burglar loudly the*. Note also that had the four words been *burglars, a, sneezes, loudly*, there is no way in which these could be combined to make a well-formed sentence. **A burglars* is an impossible combination, and so is **burglars sneezes*. In brief, English places firm restrictions on which items can occur together, and the order in which they come.

From this, it follows that there is also a fixed set of possibilities for the substitution of items. In the word *bats*, for example, *a* could be replaced by *e* or *i*, but not by *h* or *z*, which would give **bhts* or **bzts*. In the sentence *The burglar sneezed loudly*, the word *burglar* could be replaced by *cat, butcher, robber*, or even (in a children's story) by *engine* or *shoe* – but it could not be replaced by *into*, or *amazingly*, or *they*, which would give ill-formed sequences such as **The into sneezed loudly* or **The amazingly sneezed loudly*.

Every item in language, then, has its own characteristic place in the total pattern. It can combine with certain specified items, and be replaced by others (Figure 2.1).

```
The    –   burglar   –   sneezed   –   loudly
 |          |             |             |
 A     –   robber    –   coughed   –   softly
 |          |             |             |
That   –    cat      –    hissed   –   noisily
```

figure 2.1

Language can therefore be regarded as an intricate network of interlinked elements in which every item is held in its place and given its identity by all the other items. No item (apart from the names of some objects) has an independent validity or existence outside that pattern. The elements of language can be likened to the players in a game of soccer. A striker, or a goal-keeper, has no use or value outside the game. But placed among the other players, a striker acquires an identity and value. In the same way, linguistic items such as *the*, *been*, *very*, only acquire significance as part of a total language network.

Structure dependence

Let us now look again at the network of interlocking items which constitutes language. A closer inspection reveals another, more basic way in which language differs from animal communication.

Look at the sentences: *The penguin squawked. It squawked. The penguin which slipped on the ice squawked.* Each of these sentences has a similar basic structure consisting of a subject and a verb (Figure 2.2).

The penguin	
It	squawked
The penguin which slipped on the ice	

figure 2.2

The number of words in each sentence is no guide whatsoever to its basic structure. Simple counting operations are quite irrelevant to language. For example, suppose someone was trying to work out how to express the past in English. They would have no success at all if they tried out a strategy such as 'Add -ed to the end of the third word'. They might, accidentally, produce a few good sentences such as:

Uncle Herbert toasted seventeen crumpets.

But more often, the results would be quite absurd:

*Clarissa hate frogs-ed.
The girl who-ed hate frogs scream.

In fact, it is quite impossible for anybody to form sentences and understand them unless they realize that each one has an inaudible, invisible structure, which cannot be discovered by mechanical means such as counting. Once a person has realized this, they can locate the component to which the past tense *-ed* must be added even if they have never heard or said the sentence before, and even if it contains a totally new verb, as in:

The penguin shramped the albatross.

In other words, language operations are **structure dependent** – they depend on an understanding of the internal structure of a sentence, rather than on the number of elements involved. This may seem obvious to speakers of English. But the rarity, or perhaps absence, of this property in animal communication indicates its crucial importance. Its presence has not been proved in any animal system (though birdsong may turn out to be structure dependent, according to some researchers).

Moreover, the types of structure dependent operations found in language are often quite complicated, and involve considerably more than the mere addition of items (as in the case of the past tense). Elements of structure can change places, or even be omitted. For example, in one type of question, the first verbal element changes places with the subject:

    1   2
[*That dirty child*] [*must*] *wash*,

has the related question

    2   1
[*Must*] [*that dirty child*] *wash?*

And in the sentence,

Billy swims faster than Henrietta.

it is generally agreed that the sentence means 'Billy swims faster than Henrietta swims', and that the second occurrence of *swims* is 'understood'.

Such sophistication is mind-boggling compared with the thirty-six cries of the vervet monkey, or even the relatively complex dances by which bees indicate the whereabouts of nectar to their colleagues.

Human language versus animal communication

So far, the main similarities and differences between human and animal communication can be summed up as follows:

Human language is a signalling system which uses sounds, a characteristic shared by a large number of animal systems. In animal communication, there is frequently a connection between the signal and the message sent, and the system is mainly genetically inbuilt. In human language, the symbols are mostly arbitrary, and the system has to be painstakingly transmitted from one generation to another. Duality and displacement – the organization of language into two layers, and the ability to talk about absent objects and events – are extremely rare in the animal world. No animal communication system has both these features. Creativity, the ability to produce novel utterances, seems not to be present in any natural communication system possessed by animals. Finally, patterning and structure dependence may also be unique language features.

To summarize: language is a patterned system of arbitrary sound signals, characterized by structure dependence, creativity, displacement, duality and cultural transmission.

This is true of all languages in the world, which are remarkably similar in their main design features. There is no evidence that any language is more 'primitive' than any other. There are certainly primitive cultures. A primitive culture is reflected in the vocabulary of a language, which might lack words common in advanced societies. But even the most primitive tribes have languages whose underlying structure is every bit as complex as English or Russian or Chinese.

But one other similarity links human language with animal communication: it is predestined to emerge. Just as frogs inevitably croak, and cows moo, so humans are prearranged for talking.

Human language is **innately guided**. Human infants are not born speaking, but they know how to acquire any language to which they are exposed. They are drawn towards the noises coming out of human mouths, and they instinctively know how to analyze speech sounds. Bees present a parallel case: they are not born equipped with an inbuilt encyclopedia of flowers. Instead, they are pre-programmed to pay attention to important flower characteristics – especially scent. So they quickly learn how to recognize nectar-filled blooms, and do not waste time flying to kites or bus-stops.

Origin of language

Language is a highly developed form of animal signalling. But there is a missing link in the chain. How, and when, did we start to talk?

Until recently, most linguists regarded this fascinating topic as outside linguistics, many agreeing with the 19th-century linguist William Dwight Whitney that 'the greater part of what is said and written upon it is mere windy talk'.

Yet suddenly, language origin has become a trendy topic. Chunks of information are being slotted into place in a giant evolutionary jigsaw puzzle whose picture is slowly emerging.

Language probably developed in east Africa, around 100,000 years ago. Three preconditions must have existed. First, humans had to view the world in certain common ways: they noticed objects and actions, for example. Second, they were able to produce a range of sounds – a spin-off of walking upright, according to one view. Third, they must have attained the 'naming insight', the realization that sound sequences can be symbols which 'stand for' people and objects.

These preconditions enabled early humans to build up a store of words. But what about linguistic 'rules', conventional word arrangements? In all probability, rules came about among early humans in much the same way as new rules emerge in any language today. Briefly, preferences tend to become habits, and habits become 'rules'.

Original language preferences possibly reflected ways in which humans view the world. Most languages put words for actions near the objects which are acted upon, for example, 'The fisherman *caught a fish*', as in English, or 'The fisherman *a fish caught*', the order preferred in, say, Turkish. So preferences to habits to rules may be a natural progression. There was probably always flexibility, which is why all languages are not the same. Eventually, an instinctive need to maintain patterns possibly overruled any desire to preserve a strict world to language link.

The role of language

But *why* did language begin? Social chit-chat, the meaningless small talk of everyday life, may have played a key role, as it does today: 'Hallo, how nice to see you. How are you? Isn't the weather terrible?' Keeping in touch via talking could have replaced the friendly grooming indulged in by primates, according to one view. It has even been called 'grooming talking'.

The use of language for persuading and influencing others has probably always been important. Yet 'information talking' – swapping news and conveying essential commands – may not be as basic as was once assumed. It is prominent primarily in public forms of language, less so in private conversations, which form the bulk of day-to-day interactions.

Language can of course be used to communicate feelings and emotions, though this aspect of language is not well developed. Humans, like other primates, can convey emotions via screams, grunts, sobs, gestures and so on. So they need language only to confirm and elaborate these more primitive signals.

These days, various other biologically less important functions of language are also found.

Humans may use language for purely aesthetic reasons. In writing poetry, for example, people manipulate words in the same way as they might model clay or paint a picture. Or they may talk in order to release nervous tension, a function seen when people mutter to themselves in anger and frustration.

This chapter has listed some important design features of language, and considered to what extent they are found in other animal communication systems. It has also mentioned some of the main purposes for which language is used.

The next chapter will outline the major directions taken by linguists over the past two centuries, as they explored the thickets of language.

Questions

1 Suggest at least three properties of language which are rare or absent in animal communication.

2 What is meant by **creativity**?

3 What is meant by **structure dependence**?

4 Work out how many ways the words *surprisingly*, *eggs*, *eat*, *elephants*, *large*, *will*, *sometimes* can be arranged to produce well-formed English sentences.

5 Suggest some reasons why people talk.

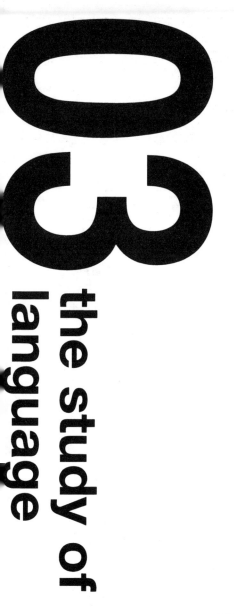

03

the study of language

This chapter sketches the main directions linguistics has taken in the past two centuries, and makes some predictions about future trends.

The discipline of linguistics can be likened to a pathway which is being cut through the dark and mysterious forest of language. Different parts of the forest have been explored at different times, so we can depict the path as a winding one.

As Figure 3.1 shows, there have been three major directions in linguistics in the past two centuries. Let us discuss each of these in more detail.

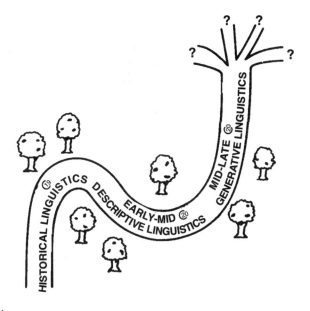

figure 3.1

Nineteenth century: historical linguistics

Before the 19th century, language in the western world was of interest mainly to philosophers. It is significant that the Greek philosophers Plato and Aristotle made major contributions to the study of language. Plato, for example, is said to have been the first person to distinguish between nouns and verbs.

1786 is the year which many people regard as the birthdate of linguistics. In that year, an Englishman, Sir William Jones, read a paper to the Royal Asiatic Society in Calcutta pointing out that Sanskrit (the old Indian language), Greek, Latin, Celtic and Germanic all had striking structural similarities. So impressive were these likenesses that these languages must spring from one common source, he concluded. Although Jones has the credit of making this discovery, it was an idea that was occurring independently to several scholars at the same time.

Sir William Jones' discovery fired the imagination of scholars. For the next hundred years, all other linguistic work was eclipsed by the general preoccupation with writing comparative grammars, grammars which first compared the different linguistic forms found in the various members of the Indo-European language family, and second, attempted to set up a hypothetical ancestor, Proto-Indo-European, from which all these languages were descended. (Figure 3.2 below excludes Hittite and Tocharian, which were not recognized as Indo-European languages until the 20th century.)

figure 3.2

The 19th-century concern with reconstructing Proto-Indo-European, and making hypotheses about the way it split into the various modern languages, was encouraged by the general intellectual climate of the times. In the mid-19th century, Darwin published his famous *Origin of Species*, putting forward the theory of evolution. It seemed natural to attempt to chart the evolution of language alongside the evolution of species.

This emphasis on language change eventually led to a major theoretical advance. In the last quarter of the century, a group of scholars centred around Leipzig, and nicknamed the 'Young Grammarians', claimed that language change is 'regular'. They argued that if, in any word of a given dialect, one sound changes into another, the change will also affect all other occurrences of the same sound in similar phonetic surroundings. For example, in Old English the word *chin* was pronounced 'kin' (spelt *cinn*). This change from a *k*-sound to *ch* affected all other *k*-sounds which occurred at the beginning of a word before *e* or *i*. So we also get *chicken, child, chide, chip, chill, cheese, cheek, chest, chew* and so on – all of which originally had a *k*-sound at the beginning. Although, today, the claims made by the Young Grammarians have been modified to some extent (as will be discussed in Chapter 13), it was an important step forward for linguists to realize that language changes were not just optional tendencies, but definite and clearly stateable 'laws' (as the Young Grammarians perhaps misleadingly called them).

The influence of the 19th-century scholars was strong. Even today, one still meets members of the general public who expect the cataloguing of linguistic changes and the reconstruction of Proto-Indo-European to be the central concern of modern linguistics.

Early- to mid-20th century: descriptive linguistics

In the 20th century, the emphasis shifted from language change to language description. Instead of looking at how a selection of items changed in a number of different languages, linguists began to concentrate on describing single languages at one particular point in time.

If any one person can be held responsible for this change of emphasis, it was the Swiss scholar Ferdinand de Saussure (1857–1913), who is sometimes labelled 'the father of modern linguistics'. Amazingly, he died without having written any major work on general linguistics. But his students collected together his lecture notes after his death and published them under the title *Course in General Linguistics* (1915), which exerted a major influence on the course of linguistics, particularly in Europe.

De Saussure's crucial contribution was his explicit and reiterated statement that all language items are essentially interlinked. This was an aspect of language which had not been stressed before. Nobody had seriously examined the relationship of each element to all the others. As noted earlier, it was de Saussure who first suggested that language was like a game of chess, a system in which each item is defined by its relationship to all the others. His insistence that language is a carefully built **structure** of interwoven elements initiated the era of **structural linguistics**.

The term 'structural linguistics' is sometimes misunderstood. It does not necessarily refer to a separate branch or school of linguistics. *All* linguistics since de Saussure is structural, as 'structural' in this broad sense merely means the recognition that language is a patterned system composed of interdependent elements, rather than a collection of unconnected individual items.

Misunderstandings sometimes arise because the label 'structuralist' is often attached to the descriptive linguists who worked in the USA between 1930 and 1960. Let us now turn to these.

In America, linguistics began as an offshoot of anthropology. Around the beginning of the 20th century, anthropologists were eager to record the culture of the fast-dying American-Indian tribes, and the American-Indian languages were one aspect of this. Although often interesting, the work of those early scholars was, for the most part, haphazard and lacking cohesion. There were no firm guidelines for linguists to follow when they attempted to describe exotic languages. This state of affairs changed with the publication in 1933 of Leonard Bloomfield's comprehensive work entitled simply *Language*, which attempted to lay down rigorous procedures for the description of any language.

Bloomfield considered that linguistics should deal objectively and systematically with observable data. So he was more interested in the way items were arranged than in meaning. The study of meaning was not amenable to rigorous methods of analysis and was therefore, he concluded, 'the weak point in language study, and will remain so until human knowledge advances very far beyond its present state'.

Bloomfield had immense influence – far more than the European linguists working during this period – and the so-called 'Bloomfieldian era' lasted for more than 20 years. During this time, large numbers of linguists concentrated on writing descriptive grammars of unwritten languages. This involved first finding native speakers of the language concerned and collecting sets of utterances from them. Second, it involved analyzing the corpus of collected utterances by studying the phonological and syntactic patterns of the language concerned, as far as possible without recourse to meaning. Items were (in theory) identified and classified solely on the basis of their distribution within the corpus.

In the course of writing such grammars, a number of problems arose which could not be solved by the methods proposed by Bloomfield. So an enormous amount of attention was paid to the refinement of analytical techniques. For many, the ultimate goal of linguistics was the perfection of **discovery procedures** – a set of principles which would enable a linguist to 'discover' (or perhaps more accurately, 'uncover') in a foolproof way the linguistic units of an unwritten language. Because of their overriding interest in the internal patterns or 'structure' of the language, such linguists are sometimes labelled 'structuralists'.

The Bloomfieldians laid down a valuable background of linguistic methodology for future generations. But linguistics also became very narrow. Trivial problems of analysis became major controversial issues, and no one who was not a linguist could understand the issues involved. By around 1950 linguistics had lost touch with other disciplines and become an abstruse subject of little interest to anyone outside it. It was ready for a revolution.

Mid- to late-20th century: generative linguistics and the search for universals

In 1957, linguistics took a new turning. Noam Chomsky, then aged 29, a teacher at the Massachusetts Institute of Technology, published a book called *Syntactic Structures*. Although containing fewer than 120 pages, this little book started a revolution in linguistics. Chomsky is, arguably, the most influential linguist of the century. Certainly, he is the linguist whose reputation has spread furthest outside linguistics. He has, in the opinion of many, transformed linguistics from a relatively obscure discipline of interest mainly to PhD students and future missionaries into a major social science of direct relevance to psychologists, sociologists, anthropologists, philosophers and others.

Chomsky has shifted attention away from detailed descriptions of actual utterances, and started asking questions about the nature of the system which produces the output.

According to Chomsky, Bloomfieldian linguistics was both far too ambitious and far too limited in scope. It was too ambitious in that it was unrealistic to expect to be able to lay down foolproof rules for extracting a perfect description of a language from a mass of data. It was too limited because it concentrated on describing sets of utterances which happened to have been spoken.

A grammar, he claimed, should be more than a description of old utterances. It should also take into account possible future utterances. In short, the traditional viewpoint that the main task of linguists is simply to describe a corpus of actual utterances cannot account for the characteristic of productivity, or **creativity**, as Chomsky preferred to call it. This, as we noted in

Chapter 2, is the ability of human beings to produce and comprehend an indefinite number of novel utterances.

Chomsky pointed out that anyone who knows a language must have internalized a set of rules which specify the sequences permitted in their language. In his opinion, a linguist's task is to discover these rules, which constitute the grammar of the language in question. Chomsky therefore used the word 'grammar' interchangeably to mean, on the one hand, a person's internalized rules, and on the other hand, a linguist's guess as to these rules. This is perhaps confusing, as the actual rules in a person's mind are unlikely to be the same as a linguist's hypothesis, even though there will probably be some overlap.

A grammar which consists of a set of statements or **rules** which specify which sequences of a language are possible, and which impossible, is a **generative** grammar. Chomsky, therefore, initiated the era of generative linguistics. In his words, a grammar will be 'a device which generates all the grammatical sequences of a language and none of the ungrammatical ones'. Such a grammar is perfectly **explicit**, in that nothing is left to the imagination. The rules must be precisely formulated in such a way that anyone would be able to separate the well-formed sentences from the ill-formed ones, even if they did not know a word of the language concerned. The particular type of generative grammar proposed by Chomsky was a so-called **transformational** one. The basic characteristics of **transformational-generative grammar** (**TGG**) are outlined in Chapters 16–18.

Chomsky not only initiated the era of generative grammars. He also redirected attention towards **language universals**. He pointed out that as all humans are rather similar, their internalized language mechanisms are likely to have important common properties. He argued that linguists should concentrate on finding elements and constructions that are *available* to all languages, whether or not they actually occur. Above all, they should seek to specify the universal bounds or **constraints** within which human language operates.

The constraints on human language are, he suggested, inherited ones. Human beings may be pre-programmed with a basic knowledge of what languages are like, and how they work. Chomsky has given the label **Universal Grammar** (**UG**) to this inherited core. He regards it as a major task of linguistics to explore its make-up.

Chomsky's recent work, his so called **Minimalist Program,** has become more and more abstract. Increasingly, he has turned to specifying broad general principles, the bare bones of human language, taking less interest in the nitty gritty details of individual tongues. He likens himself to a scientist who is content not just to watch apples dropping to the ground, but is trying to understand the principle of gravity. In this, he is following a current trend among scientists, many of whom are engaged in a 'quest for a Theory of Everything, summing up the entire universe in an equation you can wear on your T-shirt', as one mathematician expressed it.

But what happens now? Chomsky was *the* major linguistic influence for the second half of the 20th century. He still has many devoted followers. But he also has critics. They argue that Chomsky overemphasizes constraints, the bounds within which human language operates. Firm boundaries have proved quite elusive. Repeatedly, some constraint is proposed, followed rapidly by the discovery of a language which breaks it. Nor has he yet propounded a full linguistic 'Theory of Everything'.

So will the next generation continue to follow his footsteps, or is anyone breaking fresh ground?

21st century: future trends

Chomsky's influence is a permanent one. An explosion of interest in language among non-linguists has been a valuable by-product of his work. He has directed attention towards the language potential of human beings, rather than the detailed description of linguistic minutiae. As a result, huge numbers of psychologists, neurologists, anthropologists, sociologists, philosophers and others, have begun to take a greater interest in language and linguistics. Collaboration with them has led to the spiralling development of what were once 'fringe areas', such as psycholinguistics and sociolinguistics, but are now major – and still expanding – fields in their own right.

Yet alongside these developments, a quest for a less rigid framework is gathering in intensity. Of the various competitors, **optimality theory** may be leading, even though it is still in its infancy.

Optimality theory is a new major theory which suggests that there are no fixed bounds on language. Instead, Universal Grammar contains a set of violable constraints. Each language varies in its ranking of these constraints. Differences between the rankings give rise to different patterns, resulting in variation between languages.

Of course, languages mostly do not vary wildly – they cluster around statistical norms. Linguistic statisticians, and also typologists, are beginning to estimate the degree to which a construction is 'natural' both within individual languages, and within human language as a whole. Hopefully, in the next century, we will have a much firmer grasp of linguistic 'norms', and how far they can be stretched. This hunt is now aided by **corpus linguistics**, the study and use of computerized databases for linguistic research.

But alongside high level linguistic theory, day-to-day concerns about language are also being explored. Traditionally, linguists have pooh-poohed those who worry about the state of language, dismissing them as 'linguachondriacs', language hypochondriacs. Linguists maintain, as previously, that such concern is unnecessary. But they have started to pay increasing attention to attitudes towards language. They have begun to explore why pessimists hold such unfounded, gloomy beliefs, and why members of the general public are so ready to listen to them (Chapter 15). Such concerns get widely aired in debates about education, so need to be addressed.

This chapter, then, has sketched – in outline – the main directions taken by linguists in the last 200 years, and has given some pointers to future directions. The next chapter will consider how linguists today set about studying language.

Questions

1 Why were 19th-century linguists so interested in historical linguistics?
2 Why is de Saussure an important figure in linguistics?
3 What are **discovery procedures**?
4 What is a **generative** grammar, and how does it differ from a **descriptive** grammar?
5 Explain the word **explicit** when used in connection with grammars.

04
deciding where
to begin

This chapter shows that
language can be explored in
different ways, and outlines
how this book plans to
conduct the exploration.

Language is an enormous and very complex phenomenon. If one wants to study it, where should one begin? People tend to argue about this. Let us therefore consider the various possibilities. First, however, it may be useful to discuss why people disagree over the best way to go about it.

Language as a game

Language can be regarded as a complicated type of game, assuming a 'game' to be 'a specified type of activity governed by rules'. The various facets involved in a game can show why there is some argument when linguists try to decide where to begin studying language.

In a typical game, such as chess or soccer, anyone trying to find out how the game is played has to deal with three broad types of question: the *aims of the game*, the *principles of interaction*, and the *permitted moves*.

Under the **aims of the game**, comes the fundamental question: what are people trying to do when they play it? In soccer, the players are trying to kick the ball into a net in order to score. The 'aims' of language involve not only the broad functions outlined in Chapter 2 (conveying information, expressing emotion, keeping in touch socially, and so on), but also more specific purposes for which language can be used, such as:

Obtain information: *Where's the parrot?*
Make someone do something: *Shut the door!*
Make a promise: *I'll pay you next week.*

The **principles of interaction** involve questions such as: How many people can play? Do they all play at the same time, or do they take it in turns? If so, how does one know when a person's turn is over? Within language, people take it in turns to speak, and each language tends to have certain socially prescribed 'turns'. For example, in English, a greeting is usually followed by another greeting:

John: *Good morning, Felicity.*
Felicity: *Why hello there, John.*

Under **permitted moves**, linguists explore which 'moves' are permitted, and which not. In chess, some pieces can move across the board only in straight lines, and others only diagonally. With regard to language, there are rules underlying well-formed sequences of a language. In English, for example, verbs precede their objects, as in *The cat ate the canary*, rather than **The cat the canary ate* which would be the standard order in, say, Turkish.

All of these aspects of a game are important, and no one could play the game without some acquaintance with them. In language also, all these facets are relevant, and native speakers have a firm knowledge of them.

When dealing with language, one might at first sight want to tackle these facets in the order listed above. But in practice, there is a problem. It is easier to specify the basic permitted moves than it is to give an equivalent account of the aims and principles of interaction, which are closely interwoven with the social structures of the society involved. For this reason, the majority of professional linguists prefer to begin with those aspects of language which can most easily be detached from the social background. They therefore start with the permitted moves or, in linguistic terminology, the grammar of the language. They consider this to be the core of linguistic study, and expect to add on its interrelationships with society at a later stage. A knowledge of the linguistic resources of a language is often a prerequisite to an intelligent discussion of how these resources are used.

In this book, therefore, we shall be moving from the basic linguistic core outwards, in other words, we shall start from the centre of the circle diagram shown in Chapter 1 (Figure 1.1), and move out to the edges later. But a decision as to where to begin does not necessarily imply an overall order of importance: people put on their socks before their shoes, but they are not necessarily attributing greater importance to socks than to shoes.

Universal and particular

Controversy does not necessarily cease even among those who agree that it is useful to begin studying language by looking at the three central components which make up a grammar: phonology, syntax and semantics (Figure 4.1). In general, people fall into one of two categories. On the one hand, there are those who want to study language because they are interested in knowing more about one particular language. Into this first category might come a teacher of French, or a missionary who had discovered a new South American language, or a person who has an American-Indian great-grandmother and wants to know more about Nootka. On the other hand, there are those who want to find out more about language as such. Into this second category come the majority of professional linguists and other social scientists – people such as sociologists, psychologists and anthropologists, who need to know about the phenomenon of language as a whole.

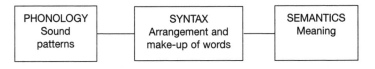

figure 4.1

These two groups of people are likely to write very different types of grammar, and to view linguistics quite differently. Those interested in a particular language will be trying to write a perfect grammar of that language (or one section of it), usually by making a detailed study of the patterns of that language alone. For example, they might be interested in the relationship of French vowels to one another. It would be quite irrelevant to them whether this vowel system coincided with that of any other language, and such people would probably pick those aspects of linguistics to help them which seemed to be best suited to the phenomenon they were examining, even if it meant choosing an unfashionable or unknown model of grammar. They are likely to consider that the chief role of linguistics is the development of analytic techniques which will enable them to fulfil their chosen task.

Those interested in language as a whole, on the other hand, will be trying to lay down a grammatical framework which will be suitable for all languages. Although such people may well write a grammar of a particular language, they will be doing this in order to test out a theory with wider implications, since one way of testing a proposed universal framework is to see whether it will fit any given language. If it does not, then it must be amended or abandoned. This type of person might also be working on French vowels, but they would be interested not so much in the vowels themselves, as in finding a framework which could 'capture' their peculiarities alongside those of other languages. A framework which was perfect for French, but was inadequate for, say, Greek, Swahili and Icelandic, would have to be abandoned.

Unfortunately, in recent years, extremists from each of these groups of people have spent an unnecessary amount of time attacking one another. Those interested in a particular language have argued that those searching for a universal framework are too theoretical and irrelevant to everyday life. One hears comments such as, 'Modern linguistics doesn't help me very much when it comes to teaching my Spanish class', and 'I'm doing a thesis on fish imagery in Shakespeare, and I can't see where linguistics fits in'. The 'universalists' counter this criticism by saying that the 'particularists' are narrow-minded people who simply like collecting facts, and one hears comments such as, 'I wish she'd stop making lists of irregular verbs in Arawak and get on with something useful'.

As will be clear from Chapter 3, the reasons for this controversy are partly historical. It is characteristic of an academic discipline to take new turnings: the 'old' school will regard the new with suspicion and distaste, and the 'new' will condemn the old as misguided and out of date. Since those who are interested in individual languages have very similar aims to the Bloomfieldian descriptivists, they tend to be treated as old-fashioned by the universalists, who are often convinced that they are 'right' merely because their type of linguistics is currently more fashionable.

In fact, the universalist and particularist views are complementary, not contradictory. No one can work seriously on a universal framework unless they have at their disposal a considerable amount of information about individual languages against which to test their theories. Conversely, the heaping up of masses of information about diverse languages reduces linguistics to the level of a hobby such as stamp-collecting unless some attempt is made to relate the miscellaneous facts within a wider framework.

Moreover, it is perhaps wrong to assume that anyone interested in linguistics *must* fall into either the particularist or the universalist category. Nowadays, a growing number of people are carrying out both types of study. In addition, those who start out with an interest in a particular language ideally move on to becoming interested in language as such. The progression from a predilection for, say, German word formation or French vowels, to a desire to help develop a universal grammatical framework can be likened to the possible progression of an intelligent motor mechanic, who is likely to move from a wish to service their own car, to an interest in how cars work in general. A person may, initially, want to learn only how to fit a new fanbelt onto a vintage Rolls-Royce. This may lead them to an interest in identifying and labelling the various components of the car's engine, and an understanding of how they fit together. Eventually, they may become curious as to how the Rolls-Royce compares with other cars, and to start looking into the theory of the internal-combustion engine as a whole.

The progression from the particular to the universal is perhaps more important for the linguist than for the motor mechanic. Anyone working seriously on a language is likely to need to know whether the phenomena they meet are unique or commonplace. To take a trivial example, someone working on English may be intrigued by the division of nouns into those that can be counted, as in *six hens*, *three cabbages*, and those that cannot: we do not normally say *six butters*, or *three soaps* (unless we mean three types of butter or soap). We have to say *some butter*, *some soap*, or use a word expressing a quantity, as in *six pounds of butter*, *three bars of soap*. How widespread is this phenomenon in the languages of the world? Is English exceptional in this respect? Or is, say, Igbo, exceptional in not having such a distinction? Furthermore, if a language *does* make this distinction, are there any other related characteristics which are likely to follow in consequence? These are the types of question which, in the short run, are likely to lead someone to study language in a wider way.

In the long run, a 'universal grammar' (if one could ever be written) would have enormously important implications for our knowledge of the human race. Such a grammar might well reflect innate properties of the human mind. In the opinion of Chomsky, 'There are very deep and restrictive principles that determine the nature of human language and are rooted in the specific character of the human mind'.

However, the idea of finding a fixed universal grammar has been slowly fading, as noted in the last chapter. Trying to find absolute constraints may be as pointless as trying to find if there is a limit on the height of human beings. It does not matter if a man 10 feet tall were to be found. What matters is understanding the normal range. Similarly, with linguistics, a search for abnormalities may not be as useful as finding out how most languages behave.

Meanwhile, ideas on any universal framework are in a continuous state of flux, particularly those of Chomsky, still the most widely worked-on theory. It is quite unrealistic to expect everyone to be aware of the latest proposed amendments, which change all the time. Because of the technical, and perhaps ephemeral nature of much recent work, this topic has been placed at the end of the book (Chapters 16–18). These chapters can be ignored by those interested only in a particular language, but are essential reading for people who want to delve further into current theories on language and linguistics.

But it is important for anyone studying linguistics to have a basic background knowledge of the techniques of descriptive linguistics, particularly the procedures and terminology used in the identification of linguistic units. The use of such techniques is essential if one is faced with a hitherto unknown, unwritten language, where the flow of speech must be broken down into segments. They can be of value in other circumstances also. Language teachers, for example, may gain new insights into the languages they teach if they approach them as if they were totally new, unwritten languages. Such people need to know the answers to such questions as: 'How can one identify words?', 'What is a word?', 'Can a word be split up into smaller segments? If so, by what criteria can one do this?', 'How is it possible to identify the basic sounds in any language?', and so on. These and similar questions will be dealt with in the next few chapters.

To return to the wheel diagram discussed in Chapter 1, we will first of all deal with the inner circles of phonology, syntax and semantics (Chapters 5–8). We will then move on to the outer rings, looking in turn at pragmatics, sociolinguistics, psycholinguistics and stylistics (Chapters 9–12). We shall then consider areas which did not fit into the circle diagram, language change and language comparison, including typology (Chapters 13–15). Finally, we shall turn to Chomsky's proposals for a universal framework (Chapters 16–18).

Questions

1 Why is language like a game?

2 Which aspects of a language are most easily detachable from social structures?

3 Why is someone working on a single language likely to want to widen out this study?

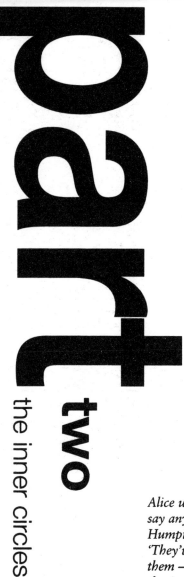

part

two

the inner circles

*Alice was too much puzzled to
say anything, so after a minute
Humpty Dumpty began again.
'They've a temper, some of
them – particularly verbs,
they're the proudest –
adjectives you can do anything
with, but not verbs – however,
I can manage the whole lot!'*

Lewis Carroll

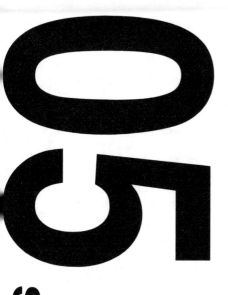

05

sound patterns

This chapter explains how linguists represent the flow of speech, and outlines the main symbols used for the sounds of English. It also discusses ways of describing stress and rhythm.

There was a young man of Dunlaoghaire,
Who propounded an interesting theoghaire,
*   That the language of Erse*
*   Has a shortage of verse*
As the spelling makes poets so weoghaire.

J.B. Searle

Linguistics is concerned primarily with the spoken word. So a priority task for anyone describing sounds is to decide how to represent the flow of speech. Clearly, the conventional written forms are most unsatisfactory, since they often provide little guide to pronunciation. The limerick quoted above suggests that Erse (Irish Gaelic) contains spelling eccentricities, and some of the idiosyncrasies of English written forms are illustrated by Bernard Shaw's somewhat exaggerated claim that *ghoti* could spell 'fish', with *gh* as in 'rough', *o* as in 'women', and *ti* as in 'station'! As de Saussure pointed out, 'Written forms obscure our view of language. They are not so much a garment as a disguise.'

Linguists, then, when they are concerned with sounds, abandon conventional spelling for the purpose of representing spoken utterances, and use one of the many specially devised systems of notation in which one symbol represents one sound. Perhaps the best known of these is the International Phonetic Alphabet (IPA). A number of IPA symbols are borrowed from the conventional written alphabet:

[b] as in '*b*ird'
[d] as in '*d*og'

(Symbols representing sounds are put into square brackets).

Other symbols are variations of alphabet letters:

[ɒ] as in 'h*o*t' is an upside down *a*.
[ŋ] as in 'ba*ng*' is a combination of *n* and *g*.
[ɪ] as in 'h*i*t' is a small-size capital I.

Sometimes obsolete letters are used:

[ʃ] as in di*sh*.

Other symbols are from the Greek alphabet:

[θ] as in *th*in,

and a few symbols are inventions:

[ɬ] Welsh *ll* as in *Ll*ane*ll*i.

Sometimes supplementary marks (known as 'diacritics') are added to the symbols. For example, two dots indicate length:

[uː] (long *u*) as in b*oo*t.

By such means, the IPA has built up a store of symbols which can, in theory, represent any sound in any language.

This book uses IPA symbols whenever a phonetic transcription is essential. However, as explained in Chapter 1, a knowledge of phonetics is considered to be prerequisite for linguistics, rather than an essential part of linguistics itself. Further information is therefore contained in an appendix (p. 244–52) rather than in this chapter. Furthermore, since phonetic symbols make a text more difficult to read, this book (in common with most other linguistic textbooks) uses the conventional written letters wherever possible, even though it is the spoken form which is being discussed.

Sorting out the basic sounds

Let us assume that a linguist is working on a hitherto unknown, unwritten language. The first step is to find a suitable informant – a reliable native speaker from whom to gather samples of speech. The early sessions will concentrate on the accurate transcription of sounds, dealing at first with single words. The linguist will do this by asking the informant to name everyday objects such as *nose, mouth, house, tree, sun,* and will then transcribe each of these words in as much detail as possible. At first even sneezes and hiccups should be recorded in case they are relevant. In Zulu, for example, there are sounds known as 'clicks' which an English speaker might well overlook, since they are totally unlike any English speech sounds. The nearest equivalents are the clicking *gee-up* sounds which people make to horses, and the *tut-tut* click of disapproval.

As time goes by, and as the sounds of the language under investigation become familiar, the linguist will transcribe more and more accurately. Simultaneously, it will slowly become apparent that the variety of strange sounds is not infinite. Instead, the informant is ringing the changes on a relatively small number of basic sounds or **phonemes**, each of which may have several variant forms.

The number of phonemes varies from language to language. The average is around thirty-five. English has forty-four, according to Gimson's well-known analysis of one widely spoken variety of British English (see Further Reading, p. 233), though different accents and different methods of analysis can result in a slightly lower number. Hawaiian, it has been claimed, has only thirteen, and one of the languages of the northern Caucasus is reported to have eighty-nine. But these extremes are unusual, and the information may be unreliable.

A **phoneme** is the smallest segment of sound which can distinguish two words. Take the words *pit* and *bit*. These differ only in their initial sound, *pit* begins with /p/ and *bit* begins with /b/. This is the smallest amount by which these two words could differ and still remain distinct forms. Any smaller subdivision would be impossible, because English does not subdivide /p/ or /b/. Similarly, take the words *pet* and *pit*. These differ only in the vowel. Once again, this is the smallest amount by which these two words could differ. There is no English sound halfway between /e/ and /ɪ/. Therefore /p/, /b/, /e/, /ɪ/ are all phonemes of English. (Symbols for phonemes are normally put into slanted brackets.) Pairs of words such as *pit* and *bit*, *pit* and *pet* which differ by only one phoneme are known as **minimal pairs**, and one way to identify the phonemes of any language is to look for minimal pairs.

The phonemes of English

Let us now list the phonemes of one widely spoken variety of British English. This is the accent sometimes known as 'Received Pronunciation' (RP). It is only one of the many accents found in Great Britain, but is perhaps the most widespread. As noted above, there are forty-four phonemes, according to one common analysis. They can be divided into two types: consonants and vowels. The latter can be subdivided into relatively **pure** or unchanging vowels, as in b*i*t, b*e*t, b*a*t, b*u*t, and **diphthongs** or gliding vowels, in which the voice glides from one vowel to another, as in b*oa*t, b*uy*, b*ay*.

Consonants

/p/ as in *p*ill
/b/ as in *b*ill
/t/ as in *t*in
/d/ as in *d*in
/k/ as in *c*ot
/g/ as in *g*ot

Vowels

/æ/ as in p*a*t
/ɑː/ as in p*ar*t
/e/ as in p*e*t
/ɪ/ as in p*i*t
/iː/ as in p*ea*t
/ɒ/ as in p*o*t

/m/ as in *m*eat
/n/ as in *n*eat
/ŋ/ as in si*ng*
/l/ as in *l*ake
/r/ as in *r*ake
/f/ as in *f*ast
/v/ as in *v*ast
/θ/ as in *th*in
/ð/ as in *th*en
/s/ as in *s*ink
/z/ as in *z*inc
/ʃ/ as in *sh*ip
/ʒ/ as in bei*g*e
/h/ as in *h*at
/tʃ/ as in *ch*in
/dʒ/ as in *g*in
/w/ as in *w*et
/j/ as in *y*et

/ɔː/ as in p*o*rt
/ʊ/ as in p*u*t
/uː/ as in b*oo*t
/ʌ/ as in b*u*t
/ɜː/ as in b*i*rd
/ə/ as in *a*go
/eɪ/ as in b*ay*
/aɪ/ as in b*uy*
/ɔɪ/ as in b*oy*
/aʊ/ as in b*out*
/əʊ/ as in b*oat*
/ɪə/ as in b*eer*
/eə/ as in b*are*
/ʊə/ as in d*oer*, d*our*

Allophones

Anyone working on an unwritten language must not only make a list of the phonemes of that language. They must also discover their variant forms or allophones. In fact, an essential part of the phoneme identification process consists of finding out which variant sounds 'belong' to each phoneme.

The amount of variation differs from phoneme to phoneme. For example, the very slight alterations in the pronunciation of English /s/ are mostly imperceptible and unimportant, whereas the variants of English /l/ are noticeable even to the untrained ear.

Sometimes the variation is random: no two sounds can ever be exactly the same, no matter how hard a speaker tries to replicate one. These slight differences normally pass unnoticed. When sounds vary randomly in this way, they are said to be in **free variation**.

At other times, the variation is predictable. The way a phoneme is pronounced can be conditioned by the sounds round it, or by its position in the word. Take the English phoneme /p/. When it occurs at the beginning of a word, it is pronounced with aspiration (a puff of breath). After /s/, this puff of breath disappears. This can be tested by holding a sheet of paper in front of the mouth and saying the words *spot, spill, pot, pill*. In the case of *spot* and *spill*, the paper remains motionless. But when *pot* and *pill* are pronounced, the accompanying puff of breath makes the paper billow out. In short, the aspirated variant [pʰ] and the unaspirated one [p] are both allophones of the phoneme /p/, and each occurs in a different and predictable set of environments. In linguistic terminology, they are in **complementary distribution**, since one set of environments complements the other.

A neat and currently fashionable way to express this is to take one variant as more basic than the other(s), and to state the circumstances under which any change in the basic form occurs. If we regard [p] as basic, we can then say that [p] changes into [pʰ] at the beginning of a word. This can be stated briefly as follows:

$p \rightarrow p^h$ /# ———. That is:

$p \rightarrow p^h$ p changes into p^h	/ in the following circumstances	# ——— after a word boundary (#) (i.e. at the beginning of a word)

figure 5.1

Or, to take another example, consider the English phoneme /l/. This has one form at the beginning of a word, and another form at the end. In a word such as *lip*, the first consonant is a 'clear' *l*, pronounced by placing the tip of the tongue just behind the teeth and keeping the back of the tongue fairly low. In *pill*, the tongue tip is in the same place, but the back of the tongue is raised, resulting in a 'dark' *l*. So the 'clear' variant [l] and the 'dark' variant [ɫ] are both allophones of the phoneme /l/. If we regard [l] as basic, we can say that [l] changes to [ɫ] at the end of a word:

$l \rightarrow ɫ$ / ——— #. That is:

l → ɫ l changes into ɫ	/ in the following circumstances	——— # when it occurs before a word boundary (#) (i.e. at the end of a word)

figure 5.2

(The distribution of these allophones is in fact more complex than the above paragraph suggests. For further information, see the books recommended on p. 233–5.)

Sound combinations

In addition to identifying and analyzing the phonemes of a language, a linguist must also work out ways in which the phonemes may be combined. Every language has certain permitted sequences of sounds, and others which are not allowed.

In English, for example, a word which begins with three consonant-type phonemes always obeys three strict rules:

1 The first phoneme must be /s/.
2 The second phoneme must be /p/ or /t/ or /k/.
3 The third phoneme must be /l/ or /r/ or /w/ or /j/.

The result is that all words beginning with three consonants are words such as *spring, string, squeal, splendid* or *stew*. We never find words such as **bdling, *sgteal* or **wbtendid*.

Shared properties of phonemes

In the discussion so far, phonemes have been regarded as separate, independent units, each one having its own allophones (Figure 5.3).

figure 5.3

It would, however, be a mistake to regard the phonemes of English as being totally separate from one another, just as it would be a mistake to regard the members of a human family as being totally different. Even though each individual in a family is a distinct person in their own right, family members are nevertheless likely to have certain genes in common with their brothers and sisters. Similarly, many phonemes share common features.

Take the English phonemes, /p/, /t/, /b/, /d/, /m/, /n/. First these all share the property of being **consonants**. Second, /b/, /d/, /m/, /n/ are all **voiced** – that is, they are pronounced with vibration of the vocal cords. If you put a hand on your Adam's apple and say the words *bet, debt, met, net*, you can feel this happening. You can also feel the vibration stopping when you get to the /t/ at the end. Third, /p/, /b/, /m/, are pronounced with the lips, and so share the property of being **labials** (from the Latin word for 'lip'). Fourth, when /m/ and /n/ are spoken, air is expelled through the nose. They are therefore both **nasals** (from the Latin word for 'nose'). And so on. The list of shared properties could continue for some time. However, linguists differ quite considerably as to which features they consider important. 'Labial', for example, is sometimes omitted, and a combination of other features used in its place.

We can draw up a chart which shows the properties possessed by each phoneme (Figure 5.4). A 'plus' sign indicates the presence of a certain property, and a 'minus' sign signifies its absence:

	/p/	/t/	/b/	/d/	/m/	/n/
Consonantal	+	+	+	+	+	+
Voiced	–	–	+	+	+	+
Labial	+	–	+	–	+	–
Nasal	–	–	–	–	+	+

figure 5.4

The more usual linguistic term for 'property' or 'component' of a phoneme is the word **feature**. So we might describe the phoneme /n/ by saying that it has the features **consonantal**, **voiced**, **nasal**. Compared with /m/, the phoneme /n/ lacks the feature **labial**. Otherwise, the two are the same. It is therefore the presence or absence of the feature labial which separates /m/ from /n/. Any feature which distinguishes one phoneme from another is called a **distinctive feature**. Since languages will, in general, have a different range of phonemes, the set of distinctive features will also tend to differ from language to language. In some cases, however, different languages are found to have the same features, but in different combinations.

This type of feature analysis makes the rules of any language much simpler to express. Suppose you had a language which dropped the phonemes /m/, /n/ and /ŋ/ at the end of a word under certain circumstances. It is simpler and clearer to write a rule which states that nasals are dropped at the end of a word than it is to name each phoneme separately. A group of sounds which share important features in common, such as the group of nasals, are known as a **natural class** of sounds.

Non-segmental phonemes

English phonemes are chunks or segments of sound, such as /b/ or /t/ or /e/. These are known as **segmental** phonemes. However, a number of languages have not only segmental phonemes, but non-segmental phonemes also.

In North Mandarin Chinese, for example, there are numerous words which are distinguished by differences in the rise and fall of tone, as in the following minimal pairs (Figure 5.5):

ma	——	(level tone)	mother
ma	/	(rising tone)	hemp
ma	∨	(dipping tone)	horse
ma	\	(falling tone)	scold

figure 5.5

Tone languages have one advantageous by-product: the tones and rhythms of speech can be imitated by instruments other than the human voice. This is the basis of African talking drums (or more accurately, talking gongs), in which the drum beats reproduce the tones and rhythms of the language. However, because the drums are unable to reproduce the segmental phonemes, their messages work in a slightly different way from normal language. A single message may take several minutes to convey, even though it would have taken only a few seconds to give the information verbally. This is because whole phrases are utilized where ordinary language uses single words. Such a procedure is necessary in order to avoid confusion. For example, among the Lokele of the Upper Congo, the word for dog is *ngwa*, a single syllable spoken with a low tone. But because there are dozens of other single syllable words spoken with a low tone, the drum equivalent for 'dog' uses a whole phrase, meaning literally 'giant dog, little one that barks kpei kpei'. The 'tune' of this phrase is unlike that of any other drum phrase, and serves to distinguish the meaning 'dog' in the message.

Metrical phonology

Although English does not have tones, it possesses important non-segmental features – characteristics which exist alongside the phonemes. In particular, each word and group of words has its own rhythm, an interplay of stressed and unstressed syllables. This branch of phonology is relatively new, and is known as **metrical phonology**.

In the words in Figure 5.6, the most stressed syllables have the most stars, and the least stressed, the smallest number of stars (some people leave the least stressed syllable unstarred, which would lower the number of stars all along):

```
    happy          happiness        unhappiness
   *    *          *   *  *          *    *   *  *
   *                *      *          *    *      *
                    *                 *    *
                                      *
```

```
        reform              reformation
        *  *                *  *    *  *
           *                *       *  *
                            *       *
                                    *
```

figure 5.6

The actual quantity of stress given to a syllable does not matter very much. The important point is the relative amount given to each. In *happiness*, for example, it is essential to give the greatest amount of stress to *hap-*, and the least to *-pi-*.

But this rhythm is not merely a sequence of different stress levels. It appears to have an internal structure, which can be represented on a 'tree diagram' – so called because its branches resemble an upside-down tree. This shows the overall structure of the rhythm better than a grid of stars. It shows how strong and weak syllables alternate, and indicates that each syllable can be regarded as a sub-portion of a larger unit, sometimes called a **foot**. The words in Figure 5.7 have been split into a strong portion (S) and a weak portion (W), which in some cases is further subdivided.

The word rhythms outlined above are not static, in that they may change as words come into contact with one another. The words *central* and *heating* each sound rather similar when pronounced alone. But when spoken together as the phrase *central heating*, the rhythm alters, so that the strongest stress goes onto *heating* (Figure 5.8).

Recent phonology pays attention not only to the interplay between words, but also to the interaction between sound segments and rhythm. For example, as in poetry, long vowels

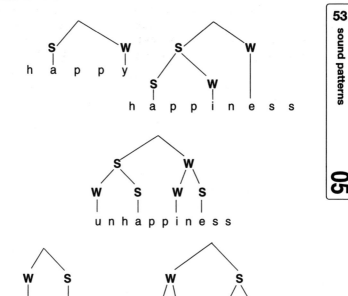

figure 5.7

tend to coincide with strong syllables, and so do short vowels followed by two consonants. In the long run, phonologists hope to work out a universal framework for handling the rhythmic structure of any language.

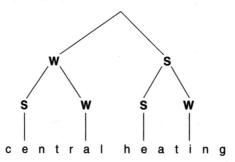

figure 5.8

This chapter has looked at how linguists handle sound structure. This is the first aspect which confronts anyone working on an unwritten language. In practice, sorting out the sound structure overlaps with the analysis of larger units, such as words. This is the topic of the next chapter.

Questions

1 What do you understand by the term **phoneme**?
2 What is a **minimal pair**? Suggest at least ten examples of minimal pairs in English.
3 What is an **allophone**? Give examples.
4 What are **distinctive features**?
5 What is a **natural class**?
6 What is **metrical phonology**?

06

words and pieces of words

This chapter looks at the problems encountered in identifying and defining the notion 'word'. It then discusses the identification and description of 'morphemes' (pieces of words). Finally, it looks at the way in which words can be assigned to 'word classes' (parts of speech).

The **word** appears to be a widespread concept. Even in primitive cultures, informants are often able to identify words. This is somewhat surprising, because nobody has yet proposed a satisfactory universal definition of the notion 'word', or provided a foolproof method of identification. People sometimes wrongly assume that a word is recognizable because it represents a 'single piece of meaning'. But it can easily be shown that this view is wrong by looking at the lack of correspondence between words from different languages. In English, the three words *cycle repair outfit* correspond to one in German, *Fahrradreparaturwerkzeuge*. Or the six words *He used to live in Rome* are translated by two in Latin, *Romae habitabat*. And even in English, a word such as *walked* includes at least two pieces of meaning, 'walk' and 'past tense'.

This chapter will deal with this matter. First, it will look at the problems of defining and identifying **words**. Second, it will consider pieces of words, or **morphemes**.

Defining words

The best-known definition of a word is that proposed by the American linguist Bloomfield, who defined it as a **minimum free form,** that is, the smallest form that can occur by itself. This is fairly unsatisfactory, because words do not normally occur by themselves in spoken speech. Even if you ask a simple question, a normal-sounding reply often requires more than one word:

Who did that?   John did.
What's that?   An oak tree.

Furthermore, some apparent words, such as *did, the, and,* are found alone only in exceptional circumstances, such as in answer to the question: 'What does *a-n-d* spell?'

Bloomfield's definition works best for written English, where we conventionally leave a space on either side. But linguists are concerned primarily with the spoken word, not the written, and the two do not necessarily coincide. For example, it seems to be purely accidental that the name of a certain type of snake, a *boa constrictor*, is written as two words rather than one, or that *seaside* appears as one word, but *sea shore* as two.

Why have linguists found it so hard to find a satisfactory definition of the notion 'word'? The answer seems to be that there are different types of word. Consider the rhyme:

A flea and a fly in a flue
Were imprisoned, so what could they do?
Said the flea: 'Let us fly'.
Said the fly: 'Let us flee'.
So they flew through a flaw in the flue.

At the simplest level, this rhyme contains thirty-six written words. But some of these are repeated. If we decide to leave out repeats and count the number of different words (in technical terms, count **word types** instead of **word tokens**), we come up against several problems. Should *fly* (noun) and *fly* (verb) be counted as the same, since they sound the same, or as different, because they have different meanings? Should *fly* and *flew* be regarded as the same, because they belong to the same verb, or as different because they have different forms? These problems can be solved only if we decide what kind of 'word' we are talking about. It is important to distinguish between **lexical items**, **syntactic words** and **phonological words**.

If by 'word' we mean **lexical item** (the technical term for 'dictionary entry'), then the sound sequence /flaɪ/ 'fly' represents two words, since most dictionaries have separate entries for *fly* (noun, N) and *fly* (verb, V):

fly N: an insect with two wings.
fly V: to move through the air in a controlled manner.

This is perhaps the most basic, and most abstract use of the word 'word'. However, both of these lexical items have various syntactic forms associated with them. The insect could occur as *fly* (singular) or *flies* (plural), and the verb could occur as *fly*, *flying*, *flies*, *flew*, *flown*. So if we counted the various syntactic forms as different words, the overall total would be much higher (Figure 6.1).

Lexical items	Syntactic words
fly N	fly flies
fly V	fly flying flies flew flown

figure 6.1

A further complication occurs with a lexical item such as *flaw*. This has the two syntactic forms *flaw* (singular) and *flaws* (plural). But the singular form *flaw* then has two different sound sequences associated with it, /flɔː/ before a consonant, and /flɔːr/ before a vowel (Figure 6.2):

*The flue had a **flaw** /flɔː/ which allowed the fly to escape.*
*There was a **flaw** /flɔːr/ in the flue.*

Lexical item	Syntactic words	Phonological words
flaw N	flaw	/flɔː/
		/flɔːr/
	flaws	/flɔːz/

figure 6.2

These examples show that we must not expect an exact overlap between different types of word. And in some other languages, the situation is far more complex than in English. In Latin, for example, the lexical item *rosa* 'rose' has twelve different syntactic forms. In Welsh, the initial consonant of each word varies systematically, depending mainly on the preceding sound: the word for 'father' could be *tad*, *dad*, *thad*, or *nhad*. The last lines of the chorus in a well-known Welsh hymn have three different forms of the verb meaning 'sing': *canu*, *ganu* and *chanu* – and there is a fourth possibility, *nghanu*, which the hymn omits.

Identifying words

For anyone working on an unknown language, it is important to identify these various types of word. There are two main stages in the analysis. First, finding chunks such as *fly*, *flew*, which recur as self-contained units. Second, deciding how many lexical items are covered by each chunk (as with *fly*, which covers two lexical items), and conversely, deciding how many different chunks belong to the same lexical item (as with *fly*, *flew*, where different syntactic forms belong to one lexical item).

For the first stage, finding chunks which behave as self-contained units, we look for sequences which are uninterruptible and mobile. These are useful guidelines in many languages. A sequence such as *chickens* cannot be interrupted. It is impossible to say *chick-little-ens*, or *chicken-little-s*. In addition, the sequence *chickens* can move about. It can occur next to different words, and in different parts of the sentence, as in: *Chickens lay eggs, foxes eat chickens, the chickens clucked loudly*, and so on.

To take another example, suppose we had come across the sequence *greentrousers*, and wanted to know whether this was one or more words. We would begin by looking for sentences which included any part of the sequence *greentrousers*. We might find:

Green leather trousers, Red trousers, Green shirts.

The fact that *greentrousers* can be interrupted by the word *leather* indicates that we are probably dealing with at least two words, *green* and *trousers*. This suspicion is confirmed by noting that both *green* and *trousers* occur with other words. But since *green* and *trousers* seem to be uninterruptible (we do not find *trous-green-ers*, for example), we surmise that each is a word.

At the end of this stage of the analysis, we have a rough list of 'words', though a list in which we are likely to have clumped together different lexical items which sound the same (**homonyms**), and to have separated different syntactic forms of the same lexical item.

For the second stage of the analysis, we need to consider the syntactic behaviour of these possible 'words', that is, their role in the overall sentence pattern. For example, *fly* N would show up as behaving differently from *fly* V, since each would fit into a different 'slot' in the sentences:

The fly buzzed.
Birds fly.

On the other hand, *fly* and *flew* would turn out to be somewhat similar, in that they would fit into the same general slot:

They fly home on Sunday.

They flew home on Sunday.

However, the syntactic behaviour of these different forms can be supplemented by an analysis of their make-up, or, in other words, the **morphemes** out of which they are constituted. Let us therefore go on to consider some basic facets of **morphology**.

Morphemes

The smallest syntactic unit is the **morpheme**. Morphemes vary in size. Neither syllables nor length are any guide to their identification. The essential criterion is that a morpheme cannot be cut up into smaller syntactic segments.

The sentence in Figure 6.3 has eleven morphemes:

The	sleep	walk	ing	albatross	chant	ed	a	dream	y	lullaby
1	2	3	4	5	6	7	8	9	10	11

figure 6.3

The, *albatross*, *a*, *lullaby*, are all single morphemes because none of them can be syntactically split up further. *Alba-* and *-tross*, for example, do not have any other role to play in the syntax of English: they exist only as part of the single unit, *albatross*. *Chanted* and *dreamy*, on the other hand, each consist of two morphemes: *chant* is found in words such as *chanting*, *chants*, and is also a word by itself, while *-ed* is found in *wanted*, *batted* and so on. Similarly, *sleep-walking* consists of three morphemes, because *sleep*, *walk* and *-ing* are all found elsewhere. In theory there is no upper limit to the number of morphemes per word: *antidisestablishmentarianism*, for example, has at least six: *anti-dis-establish-ment-arian-ism*.

Recognition of morphemes

Linguists identify morphemes by comparing a wide variety of utterances. They look for utterances which are partially the same (Figure 6.4):

The	dinosaur	sniff-**ed**	arrogant-**ly**	and	plodd-**ed**	for-**wards**
The	dinosaur	grunt-**ed**	loud-**ly**	and	edg-**ed**	back-**wards**

figure 6.4

The partial similarity between *sniffed*, *grunted*, *plodded* and *edged* enables us to isolate the segment *-ed*. And the partial similarity between *arrogantly* and *loudly*, and between *backwards* and *forwards* makes it possible to isolate *-ly* and *-wards*.

In Turkish, the similarity between *adamlar*, 'men', and *kadınlar*, 'women', enables one to identify a plural suffix *-lar*, and the words for 'man', *adam*, and 'woman', *kadın*. In Swahili, the overlap between:

nitasoma	I will read
nilisoma	I read (*past*)
utasoma	you will read
ulisoma	you read (*past*)

allows us to identify *soma*, 'read'; *ni*, 'I'; *u*, 'you'; *ta*, future tense; *li*, past tense.

Not all morphemes are as easily segmentable as these examples. But the identification of morphemes is done wholly by means of this one basic technique – the comparison of partially similar utterances.

Types of morpheme

Morphemes such as *albatross*, *chant*, *lullaby*, which can occur by themselves as whole words are known as **free** morphemes. Those such as *anti-*, *-ed*, *-ly*, which must be attached to another, are **bound** morphemes. Bound morphemes are of two main types. Consider the sentence:

*The owl **look-ed** up at the **cloud-y** sky.*

Superficially, both *looked* and *cloudy* have a similar make-up, consisting of one free morpheme, followed by a bound one. Yet the bound morphemes differ in nature. *-ed* on the end of *looked* is an **inflectional** morpheme, since it provides further information about an existing lexical item *look*, in this case indicating that the looking occurred in the past. Other examples of inflectional morphemes are the plural, as in *owls*, and the possessive, as in *Peter's car*. However, *-y* on the end of *cloudy* behaves rather differently. It is a **derivational** morpheme, one which creates an entirely new word. *Cloud* and *cloudy* behave quite differently and fit into different slots in the sentence. Other examples of derivational morphemes are *-ness* as in *happi**ness***, *-ish* as in *green**ish***, and *-ment* as in *establish**ment***.

In most cases, it is easy to tell the difference between inflection and derivation. Above all, inflectional endings do not alter the syntactic behaviour of an item in any major way. The word still fits into the same 'slot' in the sentence. Derivational endings create entirely new words. In addition, inflectional endings can be added on to derivational ones, but not vice-versa. That is, we find words such as *establish-ment-s*, but not **establish-s-ment*.

English has relatively few inflectional morphemes. These are on the whole easy to identify, though they sometimes present problems of analysis, as discussed below.

Allomorphs

Sometimes a morpheme has only one phonological form. But frequently it has a number of variants known as **allomorphs**.

Allomorphs may vary considerably. Totally dissimilar forms may be allomorphs of the same morpheme. *Cats*, *dogs*, *horses*, *sheep*, *oxen*, *geese* all contain the English plural morpheme.

An allomorph is said to be **phonologically conditioned** when its form is dependent on the adjacent phonemes. An allomorph is said to be **lexically conditioned** when its form seems to be a purely accidental one, linked to a particular vocabulary item.

The English plural morpheme provides excellent examples of both phonologically and lexically conditioned allomorphs. Let us look at some of these.

Phonological conditioning

The study of the different phonemic shapes of allomorphs is known as **morphophonology** – sometimes abbreviated to **morphonology**.

/-z/ /-s/ /-ɪz/ are all phonologically conditioned allomorphs of the English plural morpheme. That is, each allomorph occurs in a predictable set of environments.

/-z/ occurs after most voiced phonemes as in *dogs*, *lambs*, *bees*. (A voiced phoneme is one in which the vocal cords vibrate, as in /b/, /d/, /g/, /v/, and vowels.)

/-s/ occurs after most voiceless phonemes, as in *cats*, *giraffes*, *skunks*. (A voiceless phoneme is one in which the vocal cords do not vibrate.)

/-ɪz/ occurs after sibilants (hissing and hushing sounds), as in *horses*, *cheeses*, *dishes*.

If we take /z/ as basic, then we can say first, that /-z/ turns into /ɪz/ after sibilants (Figure 6.5), and second, into /-s/ after voiceless sounds (Figure 6.6):

ø → ɪ/ [+ sibilant] —— z. e.g. /hɔːsz/ → /hɔːsɪz/

ø → ɪ	/	[+ sibilant] —— z
zero changes into ɪ (i.e. insert ɪ)	in the following circumstances	between a sibilant and z

figure 6.5

z → s/[-voice]—. e.g. /kætz/ → /kæts/

z → s	/	[-voice] ——
z changes into s	in the following circumstances	after a voiceless sound

figure 6.6

Note that these 'rules' must be applied in the order given above. If the order was reversed, we would get forms such as *[dɪʃs] instead of the correct [dɪʃɪz] for the plural of *dish*.

Lexical conditioning

Words such as *oxen, sheep, geese* present a problem. Although they function as plurals in the same way as *cats, dogs*, they are not marked as plurals in the same way. Such lexically conditioned plurals do not follow any specific rule. Each one has to be learnt separately.

Words such as *oxen, sheep, geese* can be identified as syntactically equivalent to the *cats* and *dogs* type of plural because they fit into the same 'slot' in a sentence (Figure 6.7):

The _____ are making a lot of noise

cats
dogs
horses
oxen
sheep
geese

figure 6.7

Oxen, sheep and *geese* each contain two morphemes:

> *ox* + plural
> *sheep* + plural
> *goose* + plural

But only *oxen* is easily divisible into two:

> *ox* + /-ən/ (*-en*)

Sheep can be divided into two if a **zero suffix** is assumed. A 'zero suffix' is a convenient linguistic fiction which is sometimes used in cases of this type. It is normally written /ø/:

> *sheep* + /ø/.

There is no obvious way to analyze *geese*. At one time, linguists suggested that the plural vowel /iː/ in /giːs/ (*geese*) which replaces the /uː/ in /guːs/ (*goose*) should be regarded as a special type of allomorph called a **replacive**. And they analyzed the plural as:

> /guːs/ + /iː/ ← (/uː/).

Here the formula /iː/ ← (/uː/) means '/iː/ replaces /uː/'.

But this is rather a strained explanation. These days, most linguists simply accept that the form /giːs/ (*geese*) represents two morphemes:

> *goose* + plural

and that these two cannot be separated. And a similar explanation is required for forms such as *went, took*, which represent:

> *go* + past tense
> *take* + past tense.

Word classes

In every language, there are a limited number of types of lexical item. These different kinds of word are traditionally known as 'parts of speech', though in linguistic terminology the label **word class** is more common. Word classes are conventionally given labels, such as noun, verb, adjective.

Words are classified into word classes partly on account of their syntactic behaviour, partly on the basis of their morphological form. That is, words from the same word class are likely to fit into the same slot in a sentence, and to be inflected in similar ways. For example, the word class traditionally known as 'verb' can be recognized as a verb partly because it occurs after nouns (or phrases containing a noun), and partly because most verbs have an inflectional ending -*ed* to indicate the past:

Arabella **detested** *snails.*
Marianna **smiled.**

Careful analysis is needed, because in some cases, items which superficially appear to fit into the same slot in a sentence can turn out to be rather different in character. Consider the sentences:

Charlie ate **caviare.**
Charlie ate **well.**

At first sight, we might wrongly assume that *caviare* and *well* belong to the same word class. But a less superficial analysis reveals that they behave somewhat differently overall. If we tried altering the sentences around, we could say:

Caviare was eaten by Charlie.
What Charlie ate was caviare.

But we could not form the equivalent sentences with *well*:

* Well was eaten by Charlie.
* What Charlie ate was well.

These dissimilarities indicate that *caviare* and *well* are syntactically different, and belong to different word classes.

It is not always easy to tell how many word classes a language contains. Many traditional textbooks claim that English has eight 'parts of speech'. But this claim turns out to be based largely on old Latin grammars which were in turn translated from ancient Greek grammars, which mostly divided Greek words into eight word classes. If we look more closely, we find several discrepancies. For example, nouns and pronouns are traditionally classified as separate parts of speech, yet they have a large number of similarities:

Max *laughed.*
He *laughed.*

In fact, nouns and pronouns are more alike than the different types of word which are traditionally labelled adverbs. Words such as *quickly* and *very* are both usually classified as adverbs, but they behave quite differently:

He ran **quickly.**
*He ran **very.**

The number of word classes varies from language to language. Some word classes, such as noun and verb, may be universal. But others vary. Nouns, adjectives and verbs are on a continuum. At one end are nouns, words which maintain their identity over time, such as *tree, cat, river*. At the other end are verbs, words which signify rapid change, as in *walk, kick, push*. In the middle come properties, such as *large, beautiful, old*. In English, these form a separate word class, that of adjectives. But this is not inevitable. Some languages treat them as a type of verb, so-called **stative** verbs, ones which denote a state. Where English says:

Petronella is happy.

a language such as Chinese might say, as it were:

Petronella happies.

using a verb instead of an adjective. English also sometimes flips between verbs and adjectives. Compare the archaic *he ails* (stative verb) with the modern day *he is ill* (adjective).

Major word classes

English is sometimes considered to have four major word classes: noun (N), adjective (A), verb (V), preposition (P) (Figure 6.8).

Big	frogs	swim	under	water
A	N	V	P	N

figure 6.8

Of these four major classes, nouns, verbs and prepositions behave fairly differently from one another, though adjectives are somewhat strange, in that they have some noun-like qualities, and some verb-like ones. In *Blessed are the **brave**, brave* seems to have become a noun. And in *Mavis is **asleep**, asleep* seems fairly verb-like, since it fits into the same slot as *sleeping* in a sentence such as *Mavis is sleeping*.

It has been suggested that we should describe these four word classes in a manner parallel to the distinctive feature descriptions used for sounds, which can show shared similarities.

Noun	[+ N, − V]
Verb	[− N, + V]
Adjective	[+ N, + V]
Preposition	[− N, − V]

This seems to be a useful and economical way of capturing the similarities and differences between the major word classes.

The major word classes are known as **lexical categories**. Lexical categories contain **content** words, those with intrinsic meaning. They contrast with **functional categories**, which include 'little words' whose meaning is often difficult to specify, as *the*, *a*, which are **determiners (D)**, or the **complementizer** *that* in *I know that Paul is ill*, often abbreviated to **COMP** or **C**. These function words are important for gluing pieces of sentences together into longer syntactic patterns.

This chapter has discussed words and morphemes. These fit into larger recurring patterns, which will be the topic of the next chapter.

Questions

1 Suggest three different ways in which the word **word** might be used.

2 What is a **morpheme**?

3 Distinguish between **inflection** and **derivation**.

4 What is the difference between **phonologically conditioned allomorphs** and **lexically conditioned allomorphs**?

5 How might one identify **word classes**?

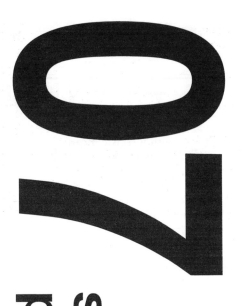

07
sentence patterns

This chapter discusses the
ways in which words can be
linked together to form larger
units. It explains how to
analyze sentences into their
'constituents' (component
parts), and shows ways of
representing this type of
analysis.

Words by themselves, or words strung together in a random way, are of relatively little use, a fact known by anyone who has visited a foreign country armed only with a dictionary, and no knowledge of the language. Does *me – bus* mean 'I am a bus', 'A bus hit me', 'I came by bus', or 'I want to go by bus'? So let us now look at how words may be combined together into longer utterances.

In this chapter, we shall consider, first, the ways in which words may be linked together to form larger units. Second, we shall discuss how to analyze sentences into their component parts, or **constituents** in linguistic terminology. Third, we shall suggest ways of representing this analysis.

Linking words together

Different languages use different devices for showing the relationship of one word to another. Most languages have one or two favourite devices. The following are especially common.

Word order

The device used most frequently in English is **word order**:

The large spider frightened Aunt Matilda.
Aunt Matilda frightened the large spider.

The words themselves in these two sentences are identical. It is the word order which indicates who frightened whom, and that it is the spider which is large, not Aunt Matilda. Languages which rely heavily on word order are known as **configurational** languages.

Inflections

In a language such as Latin, word endings or **inflections**, indicate the relationship between words. In the sentence:

Magna aranea perterruit   Matildam amitam.
Large   spider frightened Matilda   aunt
'The large spider frightened Aunt Matilda'.

the word order is irrelevant. The sentence would still mean the same if the words were arranged quite differently as in:

Magna Matildam perterruit amitam aranea.
Large   Matilda   frightened aunt   spider

The endings alone show that it was the spider which terrified Aunt Matilda, not the reverse, and that it is the spider, not Aunt Matilda, which is large. In linguistic terminology, Latin is a **non-configurational** language. Word order is not critical, though some word order preferences are found.

Function words

Another common device, used to some extent in both English and Latin, is the use of **function words**. These are words such as *of*, *by*, *that*, which indicate relationships between parts of the sentence:

*Aunt Matilda was terrified **by** a spider.*
*The Queen **of** Sheba.*
*I know **that** Penelope will come.*
*Matilda amita **ab** aranea perterrita est.*
Matilda aunt **by** spider frightened is[was]

There is some disagreement as to what counts as a function word in English. Part of the problem is that several English words, such as *to*, can be used both as a function word, and as a **content** word (one with intrinsic meaning):

*Paul wants **to** go home.* (function word)
*Peter went **to** the river.* (content word 'towards', 'as far as')

In addition, there are borderline cases, where *to* does not fit well into either type of usage:

*Andrew's suit was made **to** order.*
*It seems **to** me a good idea.*

Constituent analysis

Sentences are not simply random words strung together by means of various devices. We do not find English sentences such as:

*The large spider terrified Aunt Matilda swims of Sheba by a car.

Instead, English (like every other language) has a limited number of recurring sentence patterns. A fundamental technique of syntactic analysis is to identify these patterns by a process of successive substitution. Take the sentence:

The duck bit the burglar.

In this sentence, *the* and *duck* can be replaced by a single word such as *Donald*, *it*, without altering the basic sentence pattern. This suggests that these two words are closely linked, and together constitute a single, larger component. Similarly, the words *the* and *burglar* go together, since they also could be replaced by a word such as *Albert*, *him*. So as a first stage, we have reduced a sentence with five original components down to three more basic ones (Figure 7.1):

| The duck | bit | the burglar |

figure 7.1

Of these three components, the final two could be replaced by a single word such as *slept*. We therefore conclude that they could be bracketed together as a single, larger component. We have therefore reduced a sentence with five components down to a basic two (Figure 7.2):

figure 7.2

The linguistic procedure which divides sentences into their component parts or constituents in this way is known as **constituent analysis**. The test of substitution is basic to such an analysis, though the process is not always as straightforward as the example above.

Tree diagrams

The successive layers of constituents which make up a sentence can be shown most clearly on a **tree diagram** – so called because its branches resemble the branches of a tree. In a tree diagram, a basic sentence type at the top branches downwards in ever-increasing complexity (Figure 7.3).

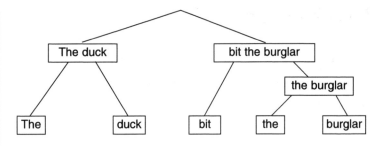

figure 7.3

The advantage of a tree diagram is that each join or **node** on the tree can be labelled, so that the whole construction becomes clearer (Figure 7.4).

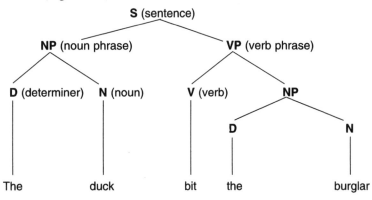

figure 7.4

A family metaphor is used to refer to the relationships on a tree (Figure 7.5). A higher node is a **mother,** and the nodes on the branches immediately beneath her are her **daughters**. Daughters of the same mother are known as **sisters**. A mother is said to **dominate** the nodes beneath her. She **immediately dominates** her daughters, but she also dominates her granddaughters, and great-granddaughters, as it were.

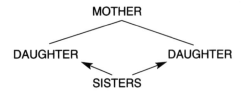

figure 7.5

Rewrite rules

An alternative way of expressing the information found on a tree diagram is by means of **rewrite** rules. A rewrite rule is a replacement rule, in which the symbol to the left of an arrow is replaced by an expanded form written to the right of the arrow.

S → NP   VP

means 'Replace the symbol S by NP VP'.

VP → V   NP

means 'Replace the symbol VP by V NP'.

NP → D   N

means 'Replace the symbol NP by D N'.

The essential structure of *The duck bit the burglar* can therefore be summarized in just three rules:

S → NP   VP
VP → V   NP
NP → D   N

On a tree diagram, these three rules would appear as in Figure 7.6.

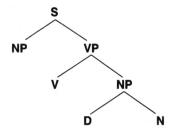

figure 7.6

These branching rules can then be supplemented by lexical substitution rules:

N → *duck, burglar*
V → *bit*
D → *the*

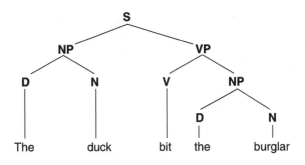

The   duck   bit   the   burglar

figure 7.7

The great advantage of rewrite rules is that they are perfectly **explicit**. They do not leave anything to the imagination. By following them, you could produce a perfect English sentence even if you did not know any English, since the rules are applied mechanically, step-by-step, one symbol at a time.

Note, however, that the above rewrite rules could also have resulted in the sentence:

The burglar bit the duck.

This does not matter, as the sequence is a perfectly good sentence of English (though admittedly a somewhat unlikely one). The rewrite rules are there to tell us what is a well-formed English sentence, not to give us information about the probable behaviour of burglars.

Identifying constituents

As we have seen, every sentence can be broken down into successive layers of constituents. However, not all sentences can be analyzed with as little trouble as *The duck bit the burglar.* Consider the sentence:

The mouse ran up the clock.

How should this be analyzed? Should we bracket [*ran up*] together, on the assumption that these words could be replaced by a word such as *climbed*? Or should we bracket [*up the clock*] together, noting that the whole phrase could be replaced by a single word such as *upwards*? Problems of this type are solved by seeing whether the groups of words in question belong together as a constituent elsewhere, since words that are grouped together in one sentence are likely to recur as a single constituent in other sentences. One way of checking this is to construct sentences in which the original words occur in a different order:

Up the clock ran the mouse.
*The mouse ran the clock up.

These sentences suggest that the words *up the clock* should be bracketed together, since they can be moved as a chunk to the front of the sentence. We may therefore analyze the sentence as:

[*The mouse*]   [*ran*]   [*up the clock.*]

and draw the tree diagram as in Figure 7.8.

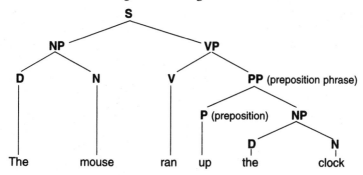

figure 7.8

The sentence discussed above must be analyzed differently from another, superficially similar sentence:

The mouse ate up the cheese.

We can show the difference by switching the sentence around:

*Up the cheese ate the mouse.
(Compare: *Up the clock ran the mouse.*)
The mouse ate the cheese up.
(Compare: **The mouse ran the clock up.*)

We may therefore analyze the second sentence as:

[*The mouse*]   [*ate up*]   [*the cheese.*]

and draw the tree diagram as in Figure 7.9, using the extra node-labels VB for 'phrasal verb' and PRT for 'particle':

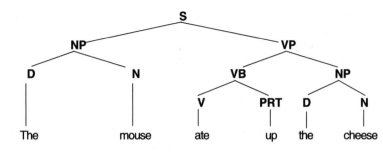

figure 7.9

Constituents behave in predictable ways, since languages ring the changes on a few recurring patterns. It is therefore possible to build up a store of specific 'tests' for the presence of a particular constituent in a given language. As *up the clock* suggests, one test for a PP (preposition phrase = phrase containing a preposition) is that a preposition cannot immediately follow its NP. Just as you cannot say:

> *The mouse ran **the clock up**.*

so you cannot say:

> *Fenella went **the woods into**.*
> *Doris swam **the bridge under**.*

Let us now go on to consider this notion of 'tests' further, by considering 'NP tests'.

NP tests

English NPs (noun phrases) recur in certain specifiable positions. Some of the main places in which they occur are:

- At the beginning of a sentence before the verb:
  ***The cat** ate the canary.*
- At the end of a sentence after the verb:
  *The canary feared **the cat**.*
- After *by* in a passive sentence:
  *The canary was eaten by **the cat**.*
- After an auxiliary verb in questions:
  *Did **the cat** eat the canary?*

Of course, other types of phrase can occur in some of these positions. But an NP such as *the cat* can occur in *all* of them. Consequently, if we find a phrase which we suspect might be an NP, we can apply these (and other) tests. For example, consider the sentences below:

> *Uncle Harry kicked the cat.*
> *Suddenly Harry kicked the cat.*

In order to find out whether the first two words in each sentence are an NP, we can apply the NP tests listed below:

- At the beginning of a sentence before a verb:
  Uncle Harry kicked the cat.
  Suddenly Harry kicked the cat.
- At the end of a sentence after a verb:
  *The cat scratched **Uncle Harry**.*
  The cat scratched **suddenly Harry.*
- After *by* in a passive sentence:
  The cat was kicked by Uncle Harry.
  The cat was kicked by **suddenly Harry.*
- After an auxiliary verb in questions:
  *Did **Uncle Harry** kick the cat?*
  Did **suddenly Harry kick the cat?*

The failure of *suddenly Harry* to pass most of these NP tests shows that it cannot be an NP, whereas the success of *Uncle Harry* indicates that it probably is an NP.

Adding in extra patterns

So far, our rewrite rules have dealt with only one structure, the pattern underlying *The duck bit the burglar*. Let us now add in some others. Consider the sentence:

> *The duck slept in the bath.*

This has the same basic division into NP VP as *The duck bit the burglar*. But the structure of the VP differs. In *The duck slept in the bath*, the verb is followed by a preposition phrase (PP) (Figure 7.10).

The extra rewrite rules required for this are:

VP → V   PP
PP → P   NP

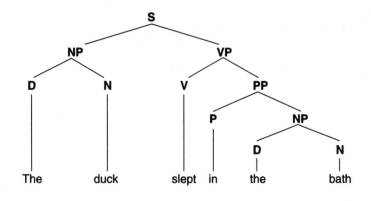

figure 7.10

However, the PP is not an essential part of the structure. It is an optional extra, since *The duck slept* is a well-formed sentence by itself. This can be shown by putting brackets round the PP in the rewrite rule, indicating that it is optional:

VP → V   (PP)

The rewrite rule above therefore underlies both *The duck slept in the bath*, and *The duck slept*. In the first, the optional PP has been selected. In the second, it has been omitted.

Let us now consider another sentence:

The burglar put the duck in a sack.

This differs from the previous structures discussed in that it is essential to have both an NP and a PP after the V (Figure 7.11). If either were omitted, the sentence would be ill-formed:

*The burglar put the duck.
*The burglar put in a sack.

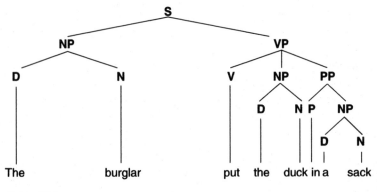

figure 7.11

The rewrite rule in this case is:

VP → V   NP   PP

So far, then, we have three different rewrite rules for English VPs:

VP → V   NP   *The duck bit the burglar.*
VP → V   (PP)   *The duck slept. The duck slept in the bath.*
VP → V   NP   PP   *The burglar put the duck in a sack.*

It would be useful to combine these three separate rules. As a first suggestion, one might simply number the types of verb (V1 for a verb such as *bit*, V2 for *slept*, V3 for *put*), and enclose them in another type of bracket { } which is used to denote alternative possibilities:

$$VP \rightarrow \left\{ \begin{array}{lll} V1 & NP & \\ V2 & (PP) & \\ V3 & NP & PP \end{array} \right\}$$

This means: 'Rewrite the VP as either V1 NP, or V2 (PP), or V3 NP PP'. However, if we wanted to include the full range of alternatives available in an English VP, the rewrite rules would become extremely long and complicated. A neater solution is to keep the rewrite rules fairly simple, and to use them in conjunction with a lexicon (dictionary) which specifies the structure associated with each V:

bit   V   [—NP]
slept   V   [—(PP)]
put   V   [—NP PP]

First, the item in question is listed, then the fact that it is a verb (V). In the square brackets come the structures associated with it. The long dash [—] indicates the place where the verb is inserted, so [—NP] says 'The verb in question must be followed by an NP'.

With these lexical entries, we need only one rewrite rule for the three types of verb:

VP → V   (NP)   (PP)

This rule says: 'A VP consists of a V optionally followed by an NP and/or a PP'. It accounts for all the possibilities discussed above, since one can slot in a verb only if it fits the structure chosen. For example, suppose we had chosen both the optional items, NP and PP, we must then slot in a verb followed by NP PP, in this case *put*. Similarly, if we had chosen V alone, the only

V which fits in this case is *sleep*.

With a detailed lexicon of this type, which can be expanded to include other word classes also, we no longer need substitution rules such as: V → *bit*, N → *burglar*.

Let us therefore summarize the rewrite rules and lexical entries for:

The duck bit the burglar.
The duck slept.
The duck slept in the bath.
The burglar put the duck in a sack.

A Rewrite rules

S   → NP   VP
VP → V   (NP)   (PP)
NP → D   N
PP → P   NP

B Lexicon

burglar	N
duck	N
sack	N
bath	N
bit	V [—NP]
slept	V [—(PP)]
put	V [—NP PP]
the	D
a	D
in	P

Of course, if more data had been considered, the rules and the lexicon would have to be complicated further. For example, if we had included a proper name such as *Donald*, the lexicon would have to specify which nouns are found with a determiner (D), as in *the duck*, *a sack*, and which not, as in *Donald* not **a Donald*. However, we set out to write rules for the sentence patterns in question, and we have done this as economically as possible.

Layers of branches

The tree diagrams we have considered so far have relatively few layers. But consider a sentence such as:

Maurice took a photograph of a platypus.

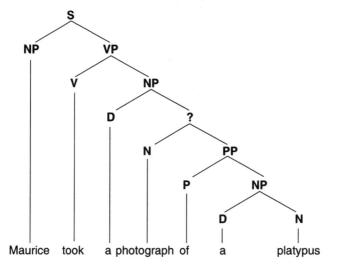

figure 7.12

The sequence *a photograph of a platypus* is clearly a noun phrase (NP) and the words *photograph* and *platypus* are nouns (N). But what of the intervening node, comprising *photograph of a platypus*? It seems to be something between an N and a full NP, so what is it? A useful solution is to give the label N̄ (pronounced N-bar, since it has a bar along the top) to something that is neither a simple N, nor a whole NP. Some people also give the label N̄ (N-double bar) to a whole NP. (In Figure 7.13, a triangle has been drawn in place of the details of the PP. This is a standard procedure which avoids wasting time and space when the details are irrelevant to the point under discussion.)

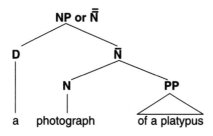

figure 7.13

The use of bars has one further major advantage: they can be used with adjectives (A), verbs (V), and prepositions (P), as well as with nouns (N). It is then easy to see similarities in structure between NPs, APs (adjective phrases), VPs and PPs which were not so evident before. It turns out that the **head** (main word) in one type of phrase is in a very similar position to the head in another. In other words, a noun in an NP is likely to be in a parallel location to an adjective in an AP, a verb in a VP and a preposition in a PP. For example, the AP *very proud of the platypus* has a structure that is similar in its branching pattern to the NP *a photograph of the platypus*. (In Figure 7.14, DEG stands for 'degree'.)

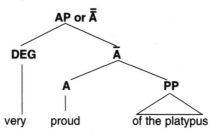

figure 7.14

A number of details still have to be worked out concerning **X-bar syntax** or **X-bar theory**, the name of this method of dealing with sentence patterns. For example, there is some controversy as to how many layers of bars it is useful to set up. But the theory appears to be here to stay, and it plays an important role in Chomsky's work.

Yet another way of handling layers has emerged in recent years, partly combined with X-bar syntax. **Functional phrases**, that is, phrases introduced by function words (Chapter 6) have a structure similar to lexical phrases, it has been claimed. For example, inflections (verb attachments) and the accompanying verb can be labelled an **inflectional phrase (IP)**. So *to fish*, *will fish*, and *fished* are all IPs. In English, the inflection, I, sometimes known as **INFL**, mostly comes before the verb, as with *to*, *will*, though sometimes after it, as with *fished* (Figure 7.15).

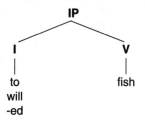

figure 7.15

Complex sentences

So far, we have assumed that all sentences are simple ones such as:

The duck bit the burglar.
The mouse ran up the clock.

In practice, however, many sentences have one or more sentence-like structures attached to them or inserted inside them. Consider:

Archibald played tennis, and Peter went fishing.

Here we have two sub-sentences of equal importance attached together to form a single one. This process is known as **conjoining**. In theory an indefinite number of sentences could be joined together:

Archibald played tennis, and Peter went fishing, and Pip played cricket, and Mary washed her hair, and Drusilla climbed the Eiffel tower…

However, conjoining is not the only process by which sentence-like structures are linked together. More often subsidiary sentences are inserted into one main sentence. This is known as **embedding** (Figure 7.16):

The rumour that the dinosaur had escaped worried the public.

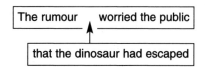

figure 7.16

In theory, a sentence can have an indefinite number of sentences embedded in it. In *The fact that the rumour that the dinosaur had escaped worried the public is not surprising*, the simple sentence has two others embedded in it (Figure 7.17).

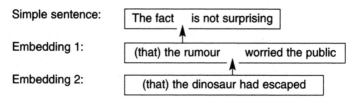

figure 7.17

Another example of embedding is the old nursery rhyme (Figure 7.18).

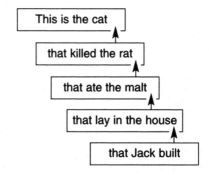

figure 7.18

Both embedding and conjoining illustrate an important property of language – that of **recursion**.

Recursion is the possibility of repeatedly re-using the same construction, so that there is no fixed limit to the length of sentences. This has important implications. It means that we can never make a complete list of all the possible sentences of any language. Instead, we must work out the system of rules which underlie the sentences.

It is quite easy to incorporate recursion into the rewrite rules, if one allows a symbol such as VP to be rewritten to include an S:

VP → V   S

This rule (which would need to be combined with the other VP rule discussed earlier) allows one to generate a sentence such as:

Mavis believes the burglar took the duck. (Figure 7.19).

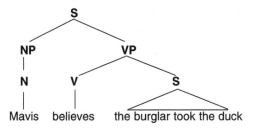

figure 7.19

So far, this chapter has shown how linguists analyze sentence patterns, with particular attention to configurational languages (those which rely on word order). There are extra problems involved in the investigation of non-configurational languages, but the notion of checking whether one constituent (component part of sentence) can be substituted for another is basic to all syntactic analyses.

Verbs: the syntax–meaning overlap

Verbs straddle the gap between syntax and semantics: the structure surrounding them provides clues to their meaning. Take the nonsense sentence:

The wickwock jipped.

Here, the wickwock has clearly done something alone, maybe jumped, or hiccuped. Or consider:

The wickwock grunched the mobe.

In this case, the wickwock has done something or other to something else.

The nouns accompanying verbs display different semantic roles, or, in more recent terminology, **thematic relations** – from the word *theme* – the label sometimes given to a noun involved in an action, though not initiating it, as in:

The snowball (theme) *rolled down the hill.*

But how many different roles are there? Some are obvious. An **agent** initiates action, and a **patient** receives it, as in:

The dog (agent) *chewed **a bone*** (patient).

A **recipient** receives something, as in:

> *Paul sent a letter to **Patsy**.*
> ***Patsy** received a letter from Paul.*

But problems arise. Consider:

> *Veronica leapt into **the water**.*

Is *the water* a **recipient**? Or is it a **goal** Veronica is aiming at? And supposing Veronica had *fallen* into the water, what then? This example shows the difficulty of deciding how many roles there are, and which one is which. The overall aim is to specify a set of relations which can be used to describe any human language, and discussions continue.

This chapter has looked at syntactic patterns, and also drawn attention to the overlap between syntax and meaning. The next chapter will discuss how linguists handle meaning.

Questions

1 Suggest three ways in which languages show the relationship of one word to another.
2 What is a **tree diagram**, and why is it useful?
3 What are **rewrite rules**?
4 Draw a tree diagram for each of the following sentences:
   The bus ran down the dog.
   The boy ran down the street.
5 Distinguish between **conjoining** and **embedding**. Give examples.
6 What are **thematic relations**?

08

meaning

This chapter explains what linguists are trying to do when they deal with 'semantics', the study of meaning. It shows that the meanings of 'lexical items' (words) are linked together in intricate lexical structures. It also outlines how the meaning of sentences might be handled.

The study of meaning is normally referred to as **semantics**, from the Greek noun *sēma*, 'sign, signal', and the verb *sēmainō*, 'signal, mean'. A linguist who is studying meaning tries to understand why certain words and constructions can be combined together in a semantically acceptable way, while others cannot. For example, it is quite all right to say:

> *My brother is a bachelor.*
> *The camel sniffed the chocolate and then ate it.*
> *The platypus remained alive for an hour after the hunter shot it.*
> *Socrates arrived yesterday.*

but not:

> !*My brother is a spinster.*
> !*The camel swallowed the chocolate and then ate it.*
> !*The platypus remained alive for an hour after the hunter killed it.*
> !*Socrates arrived tomorrow.*

These sentences are all well-formed syntactically: nouns, verbs, and so on are all in the right order. But they are contradictory. An English hearer could interpret them only by assuming that the speaker has made a mistake, in which case he would say, for instance, 'A brother *can't* be a spinster, you must mean "bachelor"'. (An exclamation mark indicates a semantically impossible sentence.)

A linguist studying semantics would also like to know why anyone who knows a language can recognize certain phrases and sentences as having similar meanings, and would ask how it is that people can recognize:

> *Indicate to me the route to my habitual abode,*
> *I am fatigued and I wish to retire,*
> *I imbibed a small amount of alcohol approximately 60 minutes ago,*
> *And it has flowed into my cerebellum.*

as roughly equivalent to:

> *Show me the way to go home,*
> *I'm tired and I want to go to bed,*
> *I had a little drink about an hour ago,*
> *And it's gone right to my head.*

A further human ability which needs explaining is the fact that hearers not only recognize ambiguous sentences, but they can also use the surrounding context to choose the most likely of the possible interpretations. For example:

Visiting great-aunts can be a nuisance.

is ambiguous. Are the great-aunts coming to see us, or are we going to see them? But if someone came across the sentence:

Visiting great-aunts can be a nuisance: I wish we didn't have to go.

they would have no doubt that we are visiting the great-aunts, rather than vice versa.

Word meaning

Clearly, the question of meaning is to a large extent connected with the meaning of individual words, or (more accurately) **lexical items** – since (as we saw in Chapter 6) the word 'word' can be misleading: *boa constrictor*, we noted, is two written words, but a single lexical item. So in a sentence such as:

!*My brother is a spinster.*

we need to find out about the meaning of *brother* and *spinster* in order to see why this sequence is unacceptable.

Three preliminary points need to be clarified in connection with word meaning. First of all, we shall be concerned primarily with content words, such as *zoo*, *apple*, *jump*, *red*, rather than with function words such as *of*, *that*, *by*, *which*, whose role is mainly to show the relationship between syntactic units (though the distinction between the two is not always clear-cut).

Second, we shall be dealing only with straightforward descriptive meaning, and ignoring what is sometimes called 'emotive' meaning or 'connotation'. For example, the word *adolescent* will be taken to mean someone who is between childhood and adulthood. We shall be ignoring the fact that some people use the word to imply that the person concerned is also likely to be awkward, immature, obstinate and moody.

Third, we must be aware that meaning is double-faced. The meaning of a lexical item such as *tree* must be considered in two ways: first of all, as one element in a language system, whose 'meaning' is dependent on relationships with the other words in the system. Second, its 'meaning' is linked up with a certain class of recognizable objects in the external world (Figure 8.1).

LANGUAGE SYSTEM   **OUTSIDE WORLD**

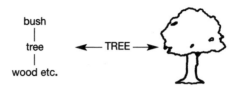

bush
|
tree ◄—— TREE ——►
|
wood etc.

figure 8.1

Linguists regard these two aspects as complementary: they examine first one, then the other, starting with the **internal** relationships between linguistic elements.

As with all linguistic elements, every lexical item has its own particular place in the pattern. By studying the relationships of individual items, linguists can build up a picture of the overall structure of a language's vocabulary. When they do this they must forget that a word such as *apple* refers to an objectively identifiable object in the outside world, and must concentrate solely on its relationships with the other items in the language.

Semantic fields

Every language cuts up the world in different ways. It is not simply that one language sometimes has more subdivisions than another in certain areas. For example, Arabic has numerous words for different types of camel, where English has a variety of words for different types of dog. The situation is far more complicated. The set of words covering a certain area in one language is unlikely to correspond to those in any other language, even when the speakers share similar cultures. This is often illustrated by the field of colour terminology. For example, Welsh and English speakers have in the past led fairly similar lives, yet Welsh *glas* traditionally covers not only the area that English speakers would call blue, but also part of green and grey as well (Figure 8.2). Nowadays, though, the traditional colour boundaries have faded and merged with the English ones.

English	Welsh
green	gwyrdd
blue	glas
grey	llwyd

figure 8.2

Yet even colour terms reflect a spuriously simple situation, since the spectrum has well-defined boundaries. More usually, we are faced with a much messier state of affairs. For example, it is impossible to translate the sentence *The cat sat on the mat* accurately into French without further information about the state of affairs described. We would have to decide arbitrarily whether the cat was sitting on a doormat (*paillasson*), a small rug (*tapis*), or a bedside mat (*descente de lit*). None of the French words corresponds exactly to our word 'mat' or 'rug' or 'carpet': *tapis* is often used to translate English 'carpet' as well as 'rug'.

These examples show us that for linguists, it is important to deal with the lexical structure of a language rather than with isolated words. The word *green* in English only becomes meaningful in relation to its neighbours in the set of colour terms: it denotes the colour between blue and yellow. Purple denotes the colour between red and blue. In semantics, as in phonology and syntax, language is not an accidental junk-heap consisting of a haphazard collection of different items. Instead, it is more like a jigsaw puzzle, where each piece fits into those which surround it, and where an isolated piece simply does not make sense if it is moved from its place in the overall pattern. We have a situation where:

every word is at home
Taking its place to support the others.

T. S. Eliot

In such a situation, it is useful to look at groups of lexical items which seem to belong together. Each item in a group or **set** can be defined by its place in relation to the other members of the set. *Adolescent* denotes someone who is no longer a child, but not yet an adult. *Cool* is the temperature between cold and

warm. For many people, *copse* refers to an entity between a tree and a wood (Figure 8.3).

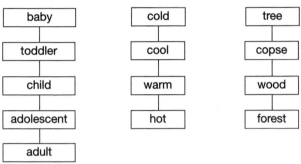

figure 8.3

Such a study can give a useful picture of the way in which a particular semantic area is divided up. It would be wrong, however, to assume that lexical items cover an entire field like a smooth mosaic. In fact, there are plenty of gaps and overlaps. In English, a gap is sometimes claimed to exist in the field of dead objects. We have a word *corpse* meaning 'body of dead human being' and *carcase* meaning 'body of dead animal', but no comparable word for a dead plant. But overlapping is perhaps the greatest problem. For example, *cow*, *princess* and *tigress* overlap in that they are all female. *Calf*, *puppy* and *baby* overlap in that they are all young and immature. *Murder*, *assassinate* and *execute* all involve the notion of killing. Let us consider how to deal with this type of problem.

Coping with overlaps

At one time, linguists hoped it might prove possible to split lexical items up into their component parts. Word meanings, like phonemes (Chapter 5), were assumed to be made up out of a stock of basic components. The word *bull* might consist of the components MALE/BOVINE/ADULT, as opposed to *cow* which would be FEMALE/BOVINE/ADULT, and *calf* which would be BOVINE/NON-ADULT. The attempt to divide lexical items into component parts is known as **componential analysis**. It feels fairly familiar because dictionaries often perform a similar type of analysis in an informal manner. For example, in the *Concise Oxford Dictionary*, *mare* is defined as 'female of equine animal'.

Componential analysis, it was thought, accounted naturally for overlaps, since one could point to components which were apparently shared by overlapping words: *cow*, *princess* and *tigress* overlapped because they shared the component FEMALE. And this type of analysis could also be extended to verbs:

die BECOME NOT ALIVE

kill CAUSE BECOME NOT ALIVE

murder INTENTIONALLY CAUSE HUMAN BEING BECOME NOT ALIVE

slaughter INTENTIONALLY CAUSE ANIMATE BEING BECOME NOT ALIVE

Unfortunately, however, it is somewhat inaccurate to speak of the meaning of words as being 'composed' out of a heap of separate components. At best, these so-called components form only a small part of the overall meaning of the word in question, and the whole approach wrongly suggests that if we looked a little more carefully, we might be able to sort out all of them. The words 'component' and 'componential analysis' have therefore faded out of fashion. Nowadays, people tend to talk of words having **semantic properties**, which is somewhat more satisfactory, since it does not imply that these properties are building blocks which need to be assembled.

Synonyms and opposites

To gain a fuller understanding of how lexical items hang together within a language, we need to look at the different types of relationship which exist between words. For example, the **synonyms** and **opposites** of a word can give valuable insights into its links with the rest of the vocabulary.

Lexical items can be regarded as synonymous if they can be interchanged without altering the meaning of an utterance:

*He **snapped** the twig in half.*
*He **broke** the twig in half.*

By studying interchangeable items, a linguist can build up a picture of those with similar meanings.

Perfect synonymy is rare. That is, it is very unusual for two lexical items to have exactly the same meanings in all contexts. Occasionally, such synonymy is found between formal and informal vocabulary items. For example, *rubella* is the term found in medical literature for the disease that is more generally known as *German measles*. But, usually, a lexical item only partially overlaps another, and the two are synonymous only in certain contexts. To return to the words *snap* and *break*:

*He **snapped** his fingers*

does not mean the same as

*He **broke** his fingers.*

And although

*He **broke** the record for the 100 metre sprint*

is an acceptable sentence,

*He **snapped** the record for the 100 metre sprint*

would seem unusual to most English speakers.

The study of opposites is more complex, as there are several different types of opposite. For this reason, the word 'antonym' has been avoided. Some writers use it for all types of opposite, others for one kind only.

The most obvious type is a pair of words in which the negative of one implies the other:

*He is **not married**: he is **single**.*
*He is **not single**: he is **married**.*

A second type of opposite is one which is not absolute, but relative to some standard. *Small* and *large*, for example, always imply some comparison:

*What a **large** mouse!* (=what a large mouse in comparison to a normal-size mouse)

*What a **small** elephant!* (=what a small elephant in comparison to a normal-size elephant)

A third type is when one word is the converse of the other. The choice of one opposite rather than another depends on the angle from which you view the situation being described:

*I **give** you the book: you **take** the book.*

Classification (inclusion)

A further way of examining lexical structure is to note the ways in which a language classifies items. In English, for example, claret and hock are classified as 'wines'. Tea and coffee are referred to as 'beverages'. And wines and beverages both come under the heading of 'drinks'.

This indicates that the vocabulary of a language is partially hierarchically structured. In Figure 8.4 below, more general items come at the top, and more specific items are subdivisions of these:

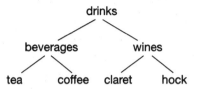

figure 8.4

The vocabulary of English is classified in this way in *Roget's Thesaurus*. Each entry has under it a list of **hyponyms** (i.e. lexical items subsumed under it). Its main drawback is that it does not distinguish between the stylistic or social variables which control the choice of synonyms.

The advantage of looking at these different relationships is firstly, they enable us to understand the multiple links between different words. Second, they can all be expressed by means of logical notation, so allowing us to be explicit in our description. Indeed, some linguists have claimed that the entire meaning of a word can be expressed in terms of its logical relationships with other words.

Fuzziness and family resemblances

So far, we have assumed that words have an agreed-upon meaning which we can discover and describe. But this is true only of some lexical items. For others, it seems to be impossible to agree upon a 'proper meaning'.

Consider the words *bachelor* and *tiger*. As a first step, we can look up these words in the *Concise Oxford Dictionary*. Here a *bachelor* is defined as an 'unmarried man'. Both unmarriedness and maleness seem to be essential properties of the word bachelor. If someone said, 'I met a bachelor and he was married', the automatic response would be 'Then he isn't a bachelor'. Or if someone said 'I know a girl who is a bachelor', the normal response would be, 'That's impossible' (unless they happened to be talking about someone who possessed a Bachelor of Arts degree). It is therefore clear that *bachelor* contains the properties MALE and UNMARRIED. This word has proved easy to analyze.

Let us now look at the word *tiger*. A dictionary definition is 'large Asian yellow-brown black-striped carnivorous maneless feline'. Which of these are essential characteristics? Presumably 'carnivorous' is not really essential, because you could say, 'Harry's tiger is not carnivorous' without getting the response, 'That's impossible, it can't be a tiger'. But what about stripiness? Here people's reactions differ. If you said 'Harry's tiger isn't striped', people's reactions fall into two categories. Some might say, 'Then it's not a tiger', indicating that stripiness is an essential part of being a tiger. But others might make a comment such as 'Well I suppose you can get albino tigers just as you get albino blackbirds', or 'Since tabby cats don't always have tabby kittens, maybe you can get unstriped tigers'. To such people, stripiness is not an essential property of tigerhood.

In brief, with some words (such as *bachelor*), there is a relatively high level of agreement as to which properties constitute an essential part of their meaning, but with others (such as *tiger*), no such agreement is found.

Fuzziness is another problem. Words often have fuzzy edges. There is no absolute divide between a cup and a mug, a glass and a vase, or a plate and a saucer. They all merge into one another. People use them inconsistently, calling something a *vase* one day, and a *glass* the next. They might call it a *vase* if it held flowers, and a *glass* if it held orange-juice.

Family resemblances create further difficulties. Sometimes a word such as *furniture* covers a whole range of things, which share characteristics with one another, as do members of a family. Yet it may be impossible to think up a set of characteristics which describes them all.

These problems indicate that it is impossible to set down fixed meanings for all words. Humans, it turns out, understand one another not by learning fixed definitions, but by working from a **prototype**, or typical example. A prototypical bird is likely to be something like a robin, with a beak, wings, stick-like legs, and an ability to fly. A penguin or an emu is still sufficiently like a bird to be regarded as a bird, even though it is not such a 'normal' or prototypical bird. This flexibility allows a great number of things to be classified as birds, even a one-legged, one-winged parrot without a beak.

It is not yet clear how to write this type of flexibility into a linguistic description. We need to pretend things are cut and dried in order to write a useful description of them; on the other hand we have to be aware that they are not. Where the balance should lie is still under discussion.

Making sense of the world

But what are these shadowy prototypes, and where do they come from? Humans, it appears, build themselves **mental models** in order to make sense of the world around them. In a simple case, as with birds, they decide which bird is the 'best' or most typical bird. But they also form ideas about more abstract concepts, often based on their own culture. English speakers regard a *week* as having seven days, divided into five working days followed by a weekend – though nothing in the external world forces this viewpoint. In other parts of the world, a week may have a different number of days. An Inca week had nine: eight working days, then market day on which the king changed his wives. Or take the word *mother*. Western parents assume that a *mother* is someone who not only gives birth to a child, but also usually looks after it and lives with the father – a culturally based picture, which is not necessarily true around the globe. Similarly, many people in England claim they live in a layered society, with upper class, middle class and working class tiers, a notion inherited from books and newspapers. And so on, and so on.

The term **mental models** was coined by psychologists for the images people construct of the world. But the phenomenon is of wide interest, and other names have been adopted. The word **representation** is preferred by those working in cultural studies. This term covers not only subconscious or inherited representations, but also those consciously put across by, say, politicians, when they invent euphemisms such as *pin-point strikes* to lead people into believing that bombs can be precisely dropped on particular targets. The use of metaphor in both propaganda and poetry will be further discussed in Chapter 12.

The meaning of sentences

So far, we have dealt only with the meaning of words. But what about sentences? In fact, the meaning of words tells us quite a lot about the meaning of sentences, since sentences are individual words linked together by means of the syntax. This enables us to understand why a sentence like:

My brother is a spinster.

is, if taken literally, contradictory. We would be saying:

My male sibling is an unmarried female.

where *male* and *female* are opposites. Some semanticists talk about such sentences as being 'false', in that they could not possibly be 'true': they deal with meaning by working out conditions under which sentences will be either 'true' or 'false'.

The amalgamation of word meaning and syntax not only enables us to reject anomalous utterances, it also allows us to make deductions about normal sentences. Take the sentence:

The cobra killed a rat.

Our knowledge that *kill* has the properties CAUSE DIE allows us to draw the conclusion that 'The rat died'. In linguistic terminology, *The cobra killed a rat* **entails** 'The rat died'. Similarly, we know that cobras are snakes, so we can conclude that 'A snake caused the rat to die', or going further: 'An animate being, a snake, a cobra, caused an animate being, a mammal, a rat to become not alive'. A large proportion of our ability to understand sentences comes from logical inferences of this type.

After a sentence has been 'unpacked' into its underlying meaning, many linguists assume that semantic representations should be expressed in some type of formal logic.

Formal logical systems can (in theory) provide formulae for the representation of the sentences of any language, and can show the logical relationships which exist between sentences. And logic has the great advantage of being able to show certain ambiguities quite clearly. Take the sentence:

All the nice girls love a sailor.

This could either mean 'Every nice girl loves some sailor or other: Alice loves Joe, Mary loves Bert, and Desdemona loves Billy'. Or it could mean 'Every nice girl loves one particular sailor: his name is Jack Tar'. Logic provides a precise notation in which the two different structures are clearly shown. At the moment, however, it is not clear which type of logic (if any, of those currently in use) is best for language.

Of course, working out logical relationships is not the only way in which humans cope with meanings. In addition, they put their common sense to work. If someone said:

That girl's an elephant.

a strict logical system would reject it as an impossibility, since girls are not elephants. But a human being would try to work out why the speaker said something so apparently idiotic. We will discuss how people do this in the next chapter.

Questions

1 How might a linguist study the internal relationships between lexical items?
2 What is **inclusion**? Give examples.
3 Distinguish three types of opposites found in language.
4 Why is it impossible to assign firm meanings to some words?
5 What is a **prototype**, and why is this notion important for the study of meaning?
6 How might one represent the meaning of sentences?

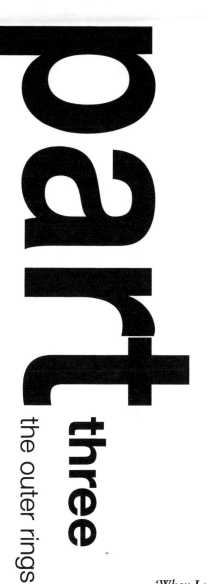

part three

the outer rings

the outer rings

'When I use a word,' Humpty Dumpty said in a rather scornful tone, 'it means just what I choose it to mean – neither more nor less.'

Lewis Carroll

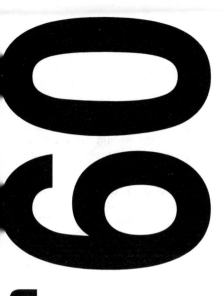

09

using language

This chapter looks at 'pragmatics', which explores aspects of meaning not predictable from the linguistic structure. It explores ways in which humans might do this, outlining the 'cooperative principle' and 'speech act theory'. It also looks at ways in which sentences might be linked together ('cohesion'), and discusses turn-taking and politeness in conversation.

'This is a self-clearing cafeteria' ran the notice in the student cafeteria. One might expect the plates and cups to put themselves away, judging from other similar phrases in the language, such as *self-cleaning oven, self-raising flour, self-righting lifeboat.* Yet the majority of students interpreted the phrase as meaning that they, the customers, were expected to clear away their plates. Why? The obvious answer is that they used their common sense and knowledge of the world to come to the most plausible interpretation in the circumstances, which was not necessarily the one which was most consistent with the linguistic structures.

Pragmatics is the branch of linguistics which studies those aspects of meaning which cannot be captured by semantic theory. In brief, it deals with how speakers use language in ways which cannot be predicted from linguistic knowledge alone. In a narrow sense, it deals with how listeners arrive at the intended meaning of speakers. In its broadest sense, it deals with the general principles followed by human beings when they communicate with one another. It is therefore sometimes light-heartedly referred to as 'the waste-paper basket of semantics'.

Pragmatics overlaps with **discourse analysis,** which deals with the various devices used by speakers and writers when they knit single sentences together into a coherent and cohesive whole.

These fields are still fairly new, and there is no general agreement yet as to how to deal with them. This chapter outlines a number of recent approaches which have proved helpful.

The cooperative principle

An American philosopher, Paul Grice, is sometimes regarded as the 'father of pragmatics'. Grice emphasized that human beings communicate efficiently because they are by nature helpful to one another. He attempted to specify the principles which underlie this cooperative behaviour, and proposed four 'maxims' or rules of conversation which can jointly be summarized as a general principle: 'Be cooperative'. These are given below.

1 Maxim of quantity

Give the right amount of information when you talk. If someone at a party asked 'Who's that person with Bob?', a cooperative

reply would be 'That's his new girlfriend, Alison'. An unco-
operative reply would be an over-brief one, such as 'A girl', or an
over-long one, such as 'That's Alison Margaret Jones, born in
Kingston, Surrey on 4 July 1980, daughter of Peter and Mary
Jones ... etc.'

2 Maxim of quality

Be truthful. For example, if someone asked you the name of an
unfamiliar animal, such as a platypus, reply truthfully, and don't
say 'It's a kookaburra', or 'It's a duck', if you know it's a
platypus.

3 Maxim of relevance

Be relevant. If someone says, 'What's for supper?', give a reply
which fits the question, such as 'Fish and chips', and not 'Tables
and chairs' or 'Buttercups are yellow'.

4 Maxim of manner

Be clear and orderly. For example, describe things in the order
in which they occurred: 'The plane taxied down the runway, and
took off to the west' rather than 'The plane took off to the west
and taxied down the runway', which might confuse people as to
what actually happened.

At this outline level, the **cooperative principle** seems like common
sense. It becomes more interesting when we consider how often
people apparently break it. In answer to the question: 'What's for
supper?' one is likely to receive a reply such as, 'Billy fell
downstairs', which doesn't answer the query. In answer to a
question: 'Why don't you like Pamela?' one might get the
response: 'Pamela's an elephant', which is patently untrue.

Such replies are not evidence against the cooperative principle.
On the contrary, they simply show how strongly it works:
people are so convinced that the other person in a conversation
is being cooperative, that a superficial breakdown in a
conversational maxim is treated as important and informative.
For example, if someone said: 'What's for supper?' and the reply
was the superficially irrelevant one: 'Billy fell downstairs', the
hearer is likely to assume that the information about Billy was
somehow important, and will fill in the gaps with assumptions
such as 'Since Billy was supposed to cook the supper, and he's
fallen downstairs, I assume that there isn't any supper ready'.

Similarly, if someone told an overt lie, such as 'Pamela's an elephant', the listener would not just think, 'That's impossible', he or she would cast around as to why the speaker had made this comment. In brief, listeners interpret what people say as conforming to the cooperative principle, even when this principle is overtly broken. They draw implications from the utterance which are not strictly there in the linguistic meaning.

The main problem with these Gricean maxims is that they are fairly vague, and the **conversational implicatures** or conclusions which can be drawn are wide and numerous. Some recent work therefore has attempted to specify how humans manage to disentangle what is relevant from the mass of possible inferences they could make.

Speech acts

When a person utters a sequence of words, the speaker is often trying to achieve some effect with those words, an effect which might in some cases have been accomplished by an alternative action. The words 'Get back!' might convey the same notion as a push. A judge's statement: 'I sentence you to five years' imprisonment' is not a mere string of words, but has the same effect as if the judge had marched a man along to a prison, and locked him up. In brief, a number of utterances behave somewhat like actions. If this line of reasoning is taken further, one could argue that all utterances are acts of some type. Even an ordinary utterance such as 'Violets are blue' might be regarded as a special type of act, the act of making a statement:

(I state that:) *Violets are blue.*

This overall approach is known as **speech act** theory, and it is another method by which philosophers and linguists have tried to classify the ways in which humans use language, in this case by treating it as parallel to other actions which humans perform.

Proponents of speech act theory try, in the first place, to list the various possible speech acts which a speaker might attempt to perform – statements, requests, queries, commands, promises, placing of bets, and so on. The lists vary from writer to writer, though the overall core tends to be similar. At the heart of the list come statements, questions and commands:

(I state that:) *It's cold.*
(I ask you:) *What's the time?*
(I command you:) *Go away!*

These are examples of **direct speech acts**: the act is expressed overtly by the most obvious linguistic means. But many speech acts are **indirect**, in that they possess the syntactic structure more usually associated with another act. For example, the following might all be intended as commands, yet only the first has the typical command structure:

> *Go to bed!*
> *Isn't it past your bedtime?*
> *You should have been in bed long ago.*

The first is therefore a direct speech act, but the second two are indirect speech acts.

But how do people know which speech act is intended, if each act can use the syntactic structure typically associated with one of the others? A possible answer is to specify **happiness conditions** or **felicity conditions** – circumstances under which it would be appropriate to interpret something as a particular type of speech act. For example, if a genuine command has been given, the hearer must be physically capable of carrying it out, and must be able to identify the object(s) involved. Even this partial statement of the felicity conditions for commands would probably enable someone to identify 'Pick up that book!' and 'That book oughtn't to be on the floor' as genuine commands, and 'Go jump in the lake!' and 'Gird up thy loins!' as pseudo-commands.

If we could fully identify the felicity conditions for each type of speech act, then we would have moved some way towards understanding how humans use language.

Remembered frameworks

The field of artificial intelligence (AI) has provided a further approach to how people understand one another. AI makes proposals about how to simulate intelligent systems on computers. The original problem was one of finding out how computers could be made to cope with inexplicit and superficially irrelevant conversations.

> Salesman: *Pink sinks are the latest fashion, madam.*
> Customer: *My dishwasher's red.*

A solution proposed for the computer might also be one utilized by humans. Knowledge, it was suggested, might be stored in the form of stereotypical situations, or **frames**. These memorized frameworks are adapted to fit in with present reality, so they are altered as required. So, for example, a person might have a frame representing a typical kitchen, and would have 'slots' in the frame for a sink, a cooker, a dishwasher and so on. A superficially disjointed conversation, such as the one above, would become quite coherent when considered in relation to the 'kitchen frame' in a person's mind. Furthermore the speakers in this conversation clearly have a certain amount of mutual knowledge, in that they both have a similar outline kitchen frame.

Another way of dealing with human interaction, therefore, is to specify both the relevant frames and the mutual knowledge held in common by the participants. These frames provide yet another way of handling representation and mental models (Chapter 8).

Discourse analysis

So far, we have concentrated on cases in which people made sense of quite strange disjointed utterances. However, when we use language, we do not necessarily do so in a random and unstructured way. Both conversation and written texts have various devices for welding together miscellaneous utterances into a cohesive whole.

A George ate the curry with delight. Curry had always been George's favourite food. The curry was subtly flavoured. George detected hints of cumin and coriander in the curry. Cumin and coriander are George's favourite spices.

B George ate the curry with delight. This type of food had always been his favourite. The dish was subtly flavoured, and in it he detected hints of his favourite spices, cumin and coriander.

The two versions are more or less the same as far as semantic content is concerned, and the syntax is fairly similar. Nevertheless, there is a lot of difference between the two. The second is both stylistically better, and more normal-sounding. The first appears to have been written sentence by sentence, without any attention to the overall effect. In the second, various devices have been used in order to link the sentences together into a cohesive whole: after its first occurrence, the word *curry* has been replaced by alternative words *this type of food, the dish*, and by the pronoun *it*. Similarly, *George* has been replaced by *he*, and in some places, the order of words has been altered so as to maintain the smooth connections, as when *in it* was brought to the front of its clause. In addition, some of the original sentences have been joined together.

Discourse analysis is the study which deals with this topic. It overlaps with **stylistics**, the study of linguistics and literature (Chapter 12). Devices which maintain the smooth flow of communication are particularly important in written language, where there is no one available to clarify unclear points. However, many of these devices are also used in ordinary conversation. Consider two versions of the same dialogue:

A Edna: *Someone ought to lock up Fred.*
Minnie: *Fred is a disgrace.*
Edna: *Someone caught Fred peeping at the new lodger through the bathroom window.*
Minnie: *What is the name of the new lodger? Is the name of the new lodger Arabella or Annabel?*

B Edna: *Fred ought to be locked up.*
Minnie: *That man's a disgrace.*
Edna: *He was caught peeping through the bathroom window at the new lodger.*
Minnie: *What's her name? Is it Arabella or Annabel?*

The first version sounds stilted and odd, even though by itself, each sentence is well-formed. The second version sounds far more like an ordinary conversation. It contains devices similar to those used in the piece of prose about George and his curry: after the first occurrence of *Fred*, the alternative phrase *that man* and the pronoun *he* was used. The third sentence has been changed into the passive, in order to keep Fred at the centre of attention. And so on. The overall result is that the whole dialogue becomes linked together into a cohesive whole, something that people who know a language do automatically – though people learning a second language usually have to be taught this skill, as the devices used vary in their details from language to language.

Taking it in turns

Mother: *And how's my pretty little darling then?*
Baby: *Ugh … Ugh.*
Mother: *O what a nice bit of wind that was! You must be feeling better!*
Baby: *Goo, goo.*

This brief snatch of 'conversation' illustrates one important fact about human speech: people take it in turns to talk. Even if one of the participants cannot speak, the other one pretends that the non-talker has taken their turn. But we can go further than simply noting the phenomenon of turn-taking. We can, in addition, describe how a typical conversation might proceed. The speakers are taking part in a social ritual partially prescribed by convention. In a dialogue, utterances very often occur in pairs, which are sometimes known as **exchanges** or **adjacency pairs**:

Question: *What's the time?*
Answer: *Ten past three.*

Greeting: *Hi, Jo.*
Greeting: *Why hallo Bill.*

Offer: *Would you like a cup of coffee?*
Acceptance: *Yes, please.*

Apology: *I'm terribly sorry.*
Minimization: *Please don't mention it.*

Paired utterances are not, of course, inevitable, and triple utterances are also frequent:

Question: *What's the time?*
Answer: *Ten past three.*
Acknowledgement: *Thanks.*

Conversations, then, typically follow a predictable format, exchanges are selected from a number of commonly used types. The options chosen by a particular speaker on a particular occasion depend on the social situation.

Repairs

Conversations do not necessarily run smoothly. People cannot always explain things properly. Or they make a mistake. Or the person they are talking to makes a mistake. These minor breakdowns, if noticed, have to be 'repaired'. So-called **repairs** can give additional insights into the way in which humans comprehend one another.

Repairs sometimes involve **self-repair**, when a speaker spontaneously notices a problem and solves it:

Could you hand me a spoon? A teaspoon, that is.
Marion arrived on Saturday – sorry, I mean Sunday.

Sometimes they involve **other-repair**, when someone is not quite sure about what has been said, or suspects that the other person has made a mistake.

> *I assume you mean a teaspoon.*
> *Did Marion really arrive on Saturday? Wasn't it Sunday?*

However, humans do not usually confront one another directly, so **other-initiated self-repair** is very common. In such cases, a listener mildly queries the speaker, who then repairs the original utterance:

> Speaker A: *Alan's taken a course in deep-sea diving.*
> Speaker B: *Alan? Has he really?*
> Speaker A: *Sorry, I don't mean Alan, I mean Alec.*

As this example suggests, humans tend to be polite to one another, so politeness can radically affect the structure of conversations. Let us consider this topic further.

Politeness

> *Shut the door!*
> *I wonder if you'd mind shutting the door?*
> *There's quite a draught in here.*

If you wanted someone to shut the door, you could in theory use any of the sentences above. But in practice, the first, a direct command, would be uttered perhaps only to a young child. To anyone else, it would seem somewhat rude. This avoidance of directness is partly culturally based: 'Why did that man look offended when I said, "Pass the salt"?' asked one puzzled visitor. She was even more bewildered when told that it would be better to say: 'I wonder if you could possibly pass the salt.' Why such a fuss, she queried, about a small quantity of salt? But in spite of cultural variation, the idea that it is politer to say things indirectly may be universal.

Humans everywhere tend to be polite in similar ways, based on two basic social requirements: 'No criticism' and 'No interference'. Humans want to be approved of, and they do not want to be imposed upon. Consequently, anyone with social know-how will minimize criticism of others and will avoid interfering with their liberty, at least overtly.

These requirements of 'No criticism' and 'No interference' have an effect on language. Any criticism or interference will be a social risk. Therefore speakers have to balance up the advantages and disadvantages of 'straight talking'. They must tot up the social distance between themselves and those they are talking to, the power relationship, the cultural norms, and make a decision.

Suppose a colleague was drinking too much whisky. The speaker could say:

Stop drinking!

but would be more likely to say tactfully:

I wonder if we should keep our heads clear for tomorrow's meeting?

Or they might even make a joke of it:

Even if everybody else goes bankrupt, the whisky manufacturers will survive!

And of course, if offending a colleague was really too much of a risk, the speaker could just have kept quiet.

But suppose someone had an urgent request, and felt obliged to impose on another person, what happens? There are various strategies which are used to soothe the situation. For example, anyone imposing is often pessimistic:

I don't suppose you could lend me a pound, could you?

Or they might try to minimize the imposition:

I won't keep you a minute, but …

Or they might just apologize:

I'm terribly sorry to bother you, but …

The various strategies occur worldwide, but they are not all necessarily found in every language. Each culture has its own preferred strategies. This type of study therefore overlaps with sociolinguistics, the topic of the next chapter.

Questions

1 What is **pragmatics**?
2 What four conversational maxims form the **cooperative principle**?
3 What is **speech act** theory?
4 What are **frames**?
5 Explain what is meant by **adjacency pairs**. Give two examples.
6 How might a polite speaker phrase a command?

language and society

This chapter is concerned with sociolinguistics, which analyzes variation within a language. It looks at differences between speech and writing, and at variation in pronunciation between different social classes. It also outlines divergence between men's and women's language. It then discusses multilingual communities and pidgins and creoles.

Sociolinguistics is often defined as the study of language and society. Whereas many linguists concentrate on discovering unity beneath the diversity of human languages, sociolinguists try to analyze the social factors which lead to this diversity. In brief, sociolinguists are interested in language differences, and especially in variation within a particular language.

The notion of a language

Perhaps the first question that a sociolinguist needs to ask is, 'What is a language?' Can the notion of 'a language' be defined geographically? Can it be equated with nationality? Or should a language be defined by the mutual intelligibility of its speakers?

The answer to all these questions appears to be 'no'. A geographical definition of a language would separate Australian, British and American English, which is obviously unsatisfactory. Nationality is a vague notion which has little to do with the language a person speaks. Numerous Soviet Jews, for example, regard themselves as essentially Jewish, yet speak Russian. Mutual intelligibility is of little help, since a Glaswegian and a cockney are likely to find it harder to understand one another than a Dutchman and a German who are considered to be speaking distinct languages. And there is no objective linguistic criterion which can be applied. Dutch and German are not only mutually intelligible, they are also structurally more alike than some of the so-called dialects of Chinese.

Faced with this dilemma, sociolinguists prefer to start with the notion of a **speech community** rather than a 'language'. And they define a speech community as any group of people who consider that they speak the same language. Consequently, Dutch and German must be regarded as separate languages, since, in spite of their similarities, the Dutch consider that they speak Dutch and the Germans consider that they speak German. And all the Chinese dialects must be classified as one language, because, in spite of far-reaching differences, their speakers all consider they speak Chinese.

Dialect and accent

Within a speech community, there is considerable language variation. The speech of its members varies according to many factors, including geographical location, age, occupation, socio-economic status, ethnic group and sex.

The most obvious type of variety in a speech community is the use of different **dialects**. A dialect is usually associated with a particular geographical area, such as the Geordie and Cockney dialects of English, which are spoken in Tyneside and London respectively. The term 'dialect' refers to far greater difference than mere pronunciation. The Lancashire dialect differs from standard British English in sound system, syntax and vocabulary, with phrases such as *I don't want for to go*, *summat* for 'something', *nowt* for 'nothing'. American English ranks as a different dialect from British English, with phonological innovations such as nasal vowels, and constructions such as 'I kinda figured maybe' and 'He said for you not to worry'.

Unfortunately, in everyday usage, the term **dialect** is often confused with the word **accent**. An accent refers only to a difference in pronunciation. A Scotsman and a Londoner are likely to speak English with different accents. But if the underlying system and the vocabulary are the same, they will be speaking the same dialect. In fact, although a considerable number of local accents are still found in Britain, dialects are dying out, due to the influence of education, radio and television.

From high to low

More interesting to sociolinguists is variation within a single geographical area. This is of two main types: variation within the speech of a single person, and variation between people. These two interact, and it is not always possible to separate them. Let us begin by considering the stylistic variation which exists in the speech of any one person.

Every native speaker is normally in command of several different language styles, sometimes called **registers**, which are varied according to the topic under discussion, the formality of the occasion, and the medium used (speech, writing or sign).

Adapting language to suit the topic is a fairly straightforward matter. Many activities have a specialized vocabulary. If you are playing a ball game, you need to know that 'zero' is a *duck* in cricket, *love* in tennis, and *nil* in soccer. If you have a drink with friends in a pub, you need to know greetings such as: *Cheers! Here's to your good health!*

In some cases, a relatively normal vocabulary is combined with altered syntax. In newspaper headlines and telegrams, all surplus words are routinely omitted, sometimes resulting in unintentional ambiguity:

Giant waves down Queen Mary's funnel (British newspaper)
Dacoits (= bandits) shoot dead policeman (Indian newspaper)

Specialized speech styles are carried to excess in some cultures, where social situations may follow a high degree of ritual, as among the Subanun, a Philippine tribe. If you want a drink, it is not sufficient simply to give the Subanun equivalent of English 'Please may I have a drink'. This utterance might cause a Subanun speaker to praise you for your fluent Subanun, but you would not get a drink! Drinking, particularly the drinking of beer, is a highly ritualized activity which progresses through a number of stages. At each stage, there is an appropriate style of speech, and advancement in Subanun society depends on how well a person copes with this.

Other types of variation are less clearcut. The same person might utter any of the following three sentences, depending on the circumstances:

I should be grateful if you would make less noise.
Please be quiet.
Shut up!

Here the utterances range from a **high** or formal style, down to a **low** or informal one – and the choice of a high or low style is partly a matter of politeness (Chapter 9).

But politeness is just one component of a more general skill, the **appropriate** use of language. Knowing *what* to say *when* is sometimes known as **communicative competence**. Native speakers just 'know' it would be odd to say 'Kindly refrain from smoking' to a 10 year-old puffing at a stolen cigarette, or rude to say 'Put that fag out' to a duchess. Both utterances are equally inappropriate. Children and foreign learners have to acquire this skill over a longish period. Lack of this type of knowledge often makes a speaker sound very funny, so much so that the use of an inappropriate register is one source of humour in English, as in:

Scintillate, scintillate, globule lucific,
Fain would I fathom thy nature specific.

This seems amusing because of the use of a formal style to 'translate' a rhyme associated with an informal nursery setting:

Twinkle, twinkle, little star
How I wonder what you are.

In England, the use of an inappropriate level of formality is not considered a serious social blunder in most instances. In any case, there is often a considerable amount of overlap between the use of the different styles. It would not matter whether you said 'Hallo' or 'Good morning' to your neighbour. In some other cultures, however, the social situation requires a far greater degree of rigidity. An extreme example is found in Java, where society is divided into three distinct social groups. At the top are the aristocrats. In the middle are the townsfolk, and at the bottom are the farmers. Each of these groups has a distinct style of speech associated with it. The top level of speech is used primarily between aristocrats who do not know one another very well, but also by a townsman if he happens to be addressing a high government official. The middle level of speech is used between townsmen who are not close friends, and by peasants when addressing their social superiors. The lowest level is used between peasants, or by an aristocrat or townsman when talking to a peasant, and between close friends on any level. Furthermore, it is the form of language used by parents to their children, so it is the style learned first by all Javanese children. However, as they grow up, children are expected to shift to addressing their parents in a more formal style, even though their parents continue to speak to them in the lowest style!

The formality–informality scale overlaps with other stylistic considerations, in particular the medium used. Let us now consider this.

Speech versus writing

Speech and writing differ in a number of ways. Consider the following spoken dialogue:

> Speaker A: *But the point is she's not such a strong character.*
> Speaker B: *It's not the point she's as str ... she's stronger than what she makes out I'll tell you now.*
> Speaker A: *Well maybe.*
> Speaker B: *She's a lot stronger cos otherwise I would have drived her mad when she lived here but no she's a lot stronger than what she makes out to you lot I'll tell you that now.*

The talk is shared between two people. They both assume some mutual knowledge, so we never hear who *she* is, or where *here* is located. It's repetitive: speaker B keeps stressing how strong *she* is.

It's not composed purely of sentences: the fragment 'Well maybe' is treated as a complete utterance. The verbs are all active ones (*tell*, *drive*, and so on), and the sentence structures are fairly straightforward. The vocabulary consists mostly of common words, with some colloquial phrases (*drive mad, I'll tell you that*).

Now look at a passage from a quality newspaper on a similar theme:

> *Assertiveness problems are pervasive. For example, marital discontent can arise from the inability of partners to talk assertively about their problems. Instead they tend to bottle up feelings, which inevitably leads to hostility. Marital violence also occurs more frequently in men low in assertiveness and may be explained by their inability to be assertive as opposed to aggressive.*

The uninterrupted flow of words is written by a single author. It is fully explicit, in that it does not refer to unexplained people or places. The only repetition is the occasional re-use of key words, such as *assertiveness, inability*. The passage contains only complete sentences. There is a passive verb *may be explained by*, and the sentence structures are relatively complex, with several embeddings (sentences one inside another, Chapter 7), as in *inability of partners to talk, tend to bottle up, which inevitably leads*. There is a spate of abstract nouns: *assertiveness, inability, discontent, violence, hostility*, and several lexical items are of fairly low frequency: *marital, pervasive*.

These passages contain fairly typical differences between spoken and written language. They can be summed up in the following table:

Spoken	Written
More than one participant	Single writer
Inexplicit	Explicit
Repetitive	Non-repetitive
Fragments	Full sentences
Simple structure	Elaborate structure
Concrete, common vocabulary	Abstract, less common vocabulary

figure 10.1

Several of these features overlap with the informality–formality scale, with speech containing informal features, and written language formal ones. Consequently, formal speech has quite a lot in common with informal writing. Readable writers are sometimes said to be those who 'write as they talk' – though this is usually an illusion, and apparent effortless spontaneity is often carefully crafted.

But the important point is this: spoken language typically involves the characteristics in the left-hand column of Figure 10.1, and written language those in the right-hand column – though each can borrow from the other. There is no hard and fast divide. A sermon is likely to have more 'written' characteristics than a chat between friends in a pub. One is not 'better' than the other, each is appropriate in certain circumstances. Written language is sometimes wrongly thought of as an ideal model for speech. In practice, those who reproduce written language when they speak sound quite odd. Occasionally, recent immigrants are regarded as pompous pedants, primarily because they may have painstakingly learned English from books.

Spoken and written characteristics, then, are another facet of speech styles which efficient speakers and writers control with ease.

Charting phonological variation

Speakers vary not only their vocabulary and syntax, but also the sound structure. Phonological variation, both between speakers and within a single speaker, is immensely important as a reflection of various social factors. Speakers of a language alter their phonology to suit a particular situation, often without realizing it. For example, someone from Devon is likely to pronounce the [r] in a word such as *farm* when chatting with friends at home, but would probably attempt to suppress it in a formal interview in London. In this case, the speaker may well be aware of the change in pronunciation. On the other hand, few speakers of standard British English realize that in informal situations they often omit the [t] at the end of words such as *last* in phrases such as *last thing*.

At one time, it was thought that such variation was fairly random, and that no precise statements could be made about it. But an American sociolinguist, William Labov, showed that this was not so. In a piece of work which has now become famous he examined the pronunciation of words such as *car, park* in New York. New Yorkers sometimes pronounce an [r] in these words, and sometimes do not. Although Labov was unable to tell which words were likely to be pronounced with [r], and which without, he found that he could predict the percentage of [r] sounds which each socio-economic class and each age group would use in any given type of speech.

Labov started his work on [r] in a highly amusing way. First, he found out which departments were on the fourth floor in three New York department stores. He then asked as many shop assistants as possible a question such as 'Excuse me, where are children's coats?' The answer to each of these queries was, of course, 'On the *fourth floor*', which included two words that could each contain an [r]. It is well-known that sales-staff tend to mimic the speech of their customers, and, as Labov predicted, he found that in the store that was considered socially inferior, the number of [r] sounds was low, under 20%. In the middle-ranking store, [r] was inserted about 50% of the time, and in the store considered socially superior, [r] was used over 60% of the time. These preliminary results clearly showed that the use of [r] in New York was a useful guide to social status.

After this preliminary survey, Labov then examined the speech of each class of person in more detail. Perhaps predictably, he found that [r] was inserted much more frequently in careful speech and in the reading of word lists than in casual speech. This was true of all social classes. There was, however, one unexpected finding. When reading word lists, lower-middle-class speakers inserted [r] more often than upper-middle-class speakers – even though in casual speech, the situation was reversed, with lower-middle-class speech containing fewer [r] sounds. This suggests that lower-middle-class speakers are more consciously aware of speech as an indicator of social class, and are making efforts to improve their status.

Phonological variation in British English

At first, one might assume Labov's results to be unique, in that they possibly reflected an American social situation that was unlikely to be paralleled elsewhere. But in England, a similar state of affairs has been found in the speech of people living in Norwich. Consider the differing pronunciations of words ending in *-ing*. Sometimes, Norwich inhabitants pronounce the *-ing* as in Standard English, and at other times they say *walkin'*, *talkin'*, *singin'*, with [n] instead of [ŋ]. When the distribution of *-ing* was examined more closely, a number of interesting facts emerged. First of all, and predictably, the proportion of *-ing* forms was much higher in careful speech than in casual speech for all social classes. For example, those classified as lower-working class used *-ing* around 70% of the time when they were asked to read word lists, but hardly ever in casual speech. On the other hand, middle-middle-class speakers used *-ing* 100% of the time in word lists, but only around 70% of the time in casual speech.

Second (and perhaps surprisingly), upper-working-class Norwich inhabitants were found to behave in a very similar way to lower-middle-class New Yorkers. For this social group, there was an enormous discrepancy between the type of speech used in word lists (*-ing* occurred 95% of the time), and that used in casual speech (*-ing* occurred only 13% of the time). Once again, speakers with a relatively low social status appeared to be attempting to 'better themselves' by speaking in a style they regarded as superior to their normal speech. The Norwich situation is illustrated in Figure 10.2 (p. 122).

A further analysis of the use of *-ing* by upper-working-class speakers revealed an unexpected sex difference. Women were found to use *-ing* more often than men. This suggests that 'changes from above' (Labov's term for changes of which speakers are consciously aware) may well be initiated mainly by women. There is further evidence that other changes are taking place 'from below', that is, below the level of conscious awareness. These changes appeared to be initiated by working-class men. For example, in Norwich, the vowel sound in words such as *night, rye, side*, is moving towards the sound *oy* [ɔɪ]. This change is furthest advanced in the speech of working-class men. It has been suggested that, perhaps unconsciously, people admire working-class men and associate them with strength and virility, and, without realizing it, adopt features found in their speech. This pattern seems not to be unique to Norwich, but a general phenomenon found in other areas of the world also.

These examples of phonological variation are highly informative. They provide an objective reflection of various social factors such as socio-economic class, ethnic group, age and sex. The effect of any one of these factors on language can be analyzed, and so can the interaction between them. For example, in one study of the interaction between ethnic group and age in Boston, a particular pronunciation of [o] was found to be associated with elderly Jews, and with Italians of all ages. The younger members of the Jewish community, who were mostly highly educated, had abandoned it, perhaps because they regarded it as non-standard. The Italians, on the other hand, tended to favour it as a mark of Italian identity. Such studies can shed interesting light on the pressures and attitudes within particular communities.

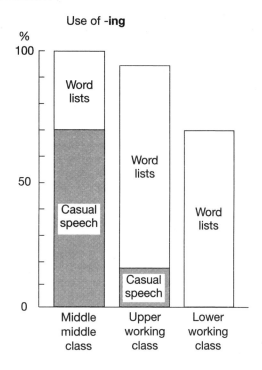

figure 10.2

Social networks

Labov-type surveys rely on collecting data from a random sample of individuals. Their speech is analyzed for various key characteristics, which are then correlated with their socio-economic background. The result, perhaps not surprisingly, suggests that human society is somewhat like a layer-cake, with different socio-economic layers stacked up on top of one another. In one respect, this is a useful insight into the way societies function. But, as with many surveys, the result is oversimplified. In practice, people do not normally live in such clearcut layers: someone from the so-called working class might well have middle-class friends and neighbours.

In fact, human beings tend to cluster into **social networks**, groups of people who regularly interact with one another. A detailed study of the social networks within one particular speech community can provide a useful corrective to Labov-type studies, which tend to suggest humans are rigidly stratified. Network studies can provide a more realistic picture of the way people interact in real life. Furthermore, if a sociolinguist manages to be introduced into a network, its members are more likely to chat in a natural way than in a Labov-type survey in which it is sometimes difficult to observe people speaking 'normally'.

The British linguists Jim and Lesley Milroy pioneered the linguistic study of social networks with a study of three communities in Belfast. Lesley was introduced into each group as 'a friend of a friend'. This ensured that she was accepted, and that people would talk relatively normally in front of her: when one youth tried to show off by talking in a somewhat affected way, his friend punched him and shouted: 'Come on, you're not on television now, you know'.

Networks can be of high density, when the same people tend to work, play and live together. On the other hand, they can be of low density, when people only have a small amount of contact with any one network, in that they may live in one area, work in another, and travel elsewhere for their social life (Figure 10.3).

When the Milroys examined their data, they discovered a number of things which would not have been detectable in a Labov-type survey. For example, Labov's work suggested that men and women's speech tended to differ, with women on the

High density network

Low density network

figure 10.3

whole being closer to the prestige norm. The Milroys found this pattern also in Belfast overall, but with some interesting subtleties. When Lesley examined the three communities separately, and charted the occurrence of the way [a] was pronounced by people of different ages and both sexes, she found some modification of the overall pattern. In the oldest, most tightly-knit, and most traditional community, she found that the predicted pattern of male–female difference was most prominent. But in the other two, which were newer, and fairly loose-knit, this pattern was less evident, and was even reversed among the younger women of one community. This suggests that a blurring of sex differentiation in language may be linked with the break-up of close-knit networks. Findings such as this indicate that linguistic variation needs to be considered from at least two angles: from the point of view of a broad Labov-type survey based on a random sample of people, but also from a close-up view of a number of social networks.

Language and sex

Possible sex differences in language usage have recently attracted a lot of attention.

First, we need to sort out whether women really do speak differently from men. People's impressions are not necessarily correct: it is often assumed, for example, that women talk more than men, whereas almost all research on the topic has demonstrated the opposite, that men talk more than women. Similarly, it is sometimes claimed that women use 'empty' adjectives, such as *divine*, *charming*, *cute*, yet this type of description is possibly more usually used by (presumably male) writers in popular newspapers to describe women.

The most consistent difference found between men and women within the western world is a tendency for women to speak in a way that is closer to the prestige standard. In colloquial terms, they speak 'better' than men. No one is quite sure why this is so, and several explanations have been proposed, which may all be partially right. For example, women may be pressurized by society to behave in a 'lady-like' manner, and 'speaking nicely' may be part of this. Or because they are the main child-rearers, they may subconsciously speak in a way which will enable their children to progress socially. Or they may tend to have jobs which rely on communication, rather than on strength. All these factors, and others, appear to be relevant. Moreover, in recent years, particularly among employed women, the differences between men's and women's speech appear to be diminishing.

Furthermore, some characteristics attributed to women turn out to be far more widespread. For example, women have been claimed to use more **hedges,** tentative phrases such as *kind of, sort of,* in place of straight statements: 'Bill is kind of short', instead of 'Bill is short'. They have also been accused of using question intonation in response to queries: 'About eight o'clock?' as a reply to: 'What time's dinner?' Yet this insecure style of conversation seems to be typical of 'powerless' people, those who are somewhat nervous and afraid of antagonizing others. Powerless people come from either sex.

But there is an alternative explanation: such speech may be **supportive.** A question intonation promotes the flow of conversation. A comment such as: 'It's cold today, isn't it?' encourages an easy-to-make response, such as: 'Yes, I even put my winter boots on'. 'Powerless' speech can therefore be viewed as friendly and cooperative, and powerful speech as insensitive and authoritarian.

Friendly speech may also reflect the setting. At a meeting, fairly formal speech is the norm. At home, or in the shops, informal conversation is more likely. Traditionally, men are more likely to be at business meetings, and women at home, though this is partly changing.

Supportive speech is more often associated with women than with men. Friendly females are likely to help the conversation along by saying 'mmm', 'aha', 'yes' – so called 'minimal responses'. These encourage the speaker, by showing that she is being listened to. Simultaneous speech can also be supportive, when the speaker's message is reinforced by the listener, as in the following overlap about going to funerals:

Speaker A: *Perhaps they would want you to go, you know ...*
Speaker B: *yeah for their comfort ...*

Such supportive speech contrasts with its opposite, power talking, whose characteristics are outlined below.

Power talking

Speaker A: *Now tell me what you're going to do.*
Speaker B: *Yes, well, first ...*
Speaker A: *Louder, please, we all want to hear.*

Speaker B: *I'd start by cutting this here.*
Speaker A: *What do you mean 'this here'?*
Speaker B: *The place where ...*
Speaker A: *Have you washed your hands?*

'Powerful' speakers typically control the topic, interrupt others, and demand explicit explanations. Occasionally, this may be justified if someone is chairing a meeting, or in some teaching situations. Yet quite often, as perhaps in the example, above, the 'controller' goes over the top, and tries both to dominate and flatten the confidence of other participants.

Power talking may be used by either sex, though it is more typically male. Male speakers not only talk more, they also interrupt more, even though they may not perceive themselves as doing so.

Men also issue more direct orders. In a study of doctor–patient interaction in the United States, men used explicit commands in about one third of the directives, as: 'Lie down', 'Take off your shoes and socks'. Women preferred to phrase commands as joint actions: 'Maybe we should just take the top of your dress off?', 'Maybe what we ought to do is stay with the dose you're on', and so on.

Change in language styles

The social situation is not necessarily static. Any change in the social relationships is likely to be mirrored in changing language styles. An example of a change of this type occurred in the gradual meaning change in the two forms of the pronouns *you* in European languages.

Originally, in Latin, there was a singular form *tu* and a plural form *vos*. For some reason (the cause is disputed), the plural came to be used as a polite form of address for speaking to a single person in authority. One theory is that when there were two Roman emperors – one in Constantinople, the other in the west in Rome – it became customary to address each of them as *vos*, since both emperors were implicitly being addressed at the same time. This began a general trend for using *vos* to anyone in authority. It gradually became customary for a working-class person to address a member of the aristocracy as *vos*, while the upper classes still used *tu* to a lower-class individual. Meanwhile, as a mark of respect, the aristocracy began to address one another as *vos*, although the lower classes continued to address one another as *tu*. This situation is shown in Figure 10.4. This linguistic situation reflected the social situation. There existed a feudal society in which the power of one class over another was all-important.

	To upper class	To lower class
Upper class	vos	tu
Lower class	vos	tu

figure 10.4

However, as feudalism died out, so did this structuring of *tu* and *vos*. Gradually (according to one theory), people ceased to feel such respect for those in power, and instead, they merely felt remote from them. *Vos* (it is claimed) came to be not so much a mark of respect, as one of non-intimacy. *Tu* came to be thought of as indicating intimacy, companionship and solidarity. People involved in friendships or close relationships started to call one another *tu* irrespective of the power situation. And this is the state of affairs today in the numerous European languages which have two forms of the word *you*.

The 'power' to 'solidarity' switch is possibly only one of several factors involved in the change from *vos* to *tu*, and some have disputed its importance. However, a similar phenomenon seems to be occurring in other parts of the world also: in India, in the Hindi and Gujarati languages, there was formerly a power pattern shown in the non-reciprocal nature of the forms of address between husband and wife, and older and younger brother. Nowadays this is dying out. Reciprocal relations are gradually becoming more important than the power of one person over another, and members of Indian families are beginning to address one another with the intimate *you* forms.

Multilingual communities

'I speak Spanish to God, Italian to women, French to men, and German to my horse', is a saying attributed to the Holy Roman Emperor Charles V. As this quotation suggests, in some cultures a changed social situation is marked by a change in the actual language spoken, a phenomenon known as **code-switching**.

Sociolinguistically, this is not very different from stylistic variation within a single language. Sociolinguists have therefore become interested in studying code-switching in bilingual and multilingual communities.

For example, in Sauris, a small community of north-eastern Italy, high in the Carnian Alps, a quite remarkable linguistic situation exists. The inhabitants use three different languages in the course of their everyday life: a German dialect, Italian and Friulian (a Romance dialect). Italian is the language of organized religion, and also that used in schools. Friulian is the language used by men in the local bars. And German is the language in the home. It is highly unusual to hear German outside the home, though it was observed on one occasion when a furious woman burst into a bar and upbraided her husband for not having returned home at the time he was expected!

A study of the ways in which these multiple languages are used is particularly important for **language planning**, a situation in which a government or education authority attempts to manipulate the linguistic situation in a particular direction. This is more likely to be successful if existing uses of a language are gradually extended, since the sudden imposition of a particular language by decree may well result in failure.

However, multilingual societies in which all the speakers are proficient in all the languages spoken are something of a rarity. Quite often, one language, or simplified language, is adopted as a common means of communication. This can happen either naturally, or as a result of language planning. A common language of this type is sometimes known as a **lingua franca**. A couple of millennia ago, Latin spread around the Mediterranean countries in this way. In India today, English tends to be a lingua franca: Hindi speakers from the north are likely to communicate in English with people from the south who mostly speak one of the Dravidian languages. The artificial language, Esperanto, is sometimes proposed as a candidate for a world lingua franca.

Pidgins and creoles

Adopting a lingua franca is not the only solution to the problem of communication between groups of people speaking different languages. In some cases, a **pidgin** develops.

A **pidgin** is a restricted language system which arises in order to fulfil essential communication needs among people with no common language. It is no one's first language, and is used at first in a limited set of circumstances. Such a system typically develops on trade routes and in coastal areas.

A pidgin is usually based on one language, though it soon acquires an admixture of other languages, as well as independent constructions of its own. For example, Tok Pisin (also known as Melanesian Pidgin English and Neo-Melanesian) which is spoken in Papua New Guinea, is based on English, and many of the words sound somewhat like English ones:

Mi go long taun. 'I go/went to the town'.
Yu wokabaut long rot. 'You walk/walked along the road'.

But there are plenty of others, which cannot be predicted from English, such as *lotu* 'church', *diwai* 'tree', *susu* 'milk'. In addition, it has acquired syntactic constructions which do not figure in English. For example, there is a consistent distinction between verbs with an object ('transitive' verbs) which take the ending *-im*, as with *bagarapim* 'wreck', and those without ('intransitive' verbs) as in *bagarap* 'collapse', 'break down':

Mi bagarapim ka bilong yu. 'I crashed your car'.
Ka bilong mi i bagarap. 'My car broke down'.

Another innovation is the particle *i* which sometimes has to be placed before the verb (as in the second sentence above).

The phonology, syntax and lexicon are simpler in a pidgin than in an ordinary language. There are fewer phonemes. In Tok Pisin, [p] and [f] are often merged, so are [s] and [ʃ], and there are only five vowels. English 'fish' was borrowed as *pis*, and English 'ship' as *sip*. In order to avoid confusion, 'piss' (urinate) became *pispis*, and 'sheep' became *sipsip*. There are very few word endings, the sentences have a simple structure, and there is a small vocabulary. One or two items stretch over a wide area, as with the following uses of the word *pikinini* 'child':

pikinini man 'son' (lit. child man).
pikinini meri 'daughter' (lit. child woman).
pikinini hos 'foal' (lit. child horse).
pikinini pis 'minnow' (lit. child fish).
pikinini bilong rais 'rice kernels' (lit. child of rice).
pikinini bilong diwai 'fruit of tree' (lit. child of tree).

Sometimes, pidgins die out of their own accord. At other times they increase in importance, and become used in more and more areas of life. If someone then acquires a pidgin as a first language – perhaps because of intermarriage between people whose only common language is the pidgin — the language has then become a **creole**.

Once it has become a creole, the system tends to develop rapidly. Speech is speeded up, the syntax becomes more complex, and extra vocabulary items are created. Fairly soon, if it continues to develop, a creole is likely to be indistinguishable from a 'full' language.

In some circumstances, however, a creole can be devoured by its parent. If a creole is spoken in an area where the base language is also used, then there may be social pressure on the creole speakers to speak the base, which often has more prestige. Therefore, little by little, the creole becomes **decreolized**, as words and constructions from the base language replace the creole ones.

The study of pidgins and creoles has grown rapidly, because their implications and interest spread far beyond sociolinguistics. They are valuable for the insights they provide into language change, and some people have claimed that they shed light on language universals – that they present language in a stripped down and basic state. This claim is controversial, but the interest it has aroused has increased the attention given to the topic. Only time will tell whether such grandiose claims are justified.

However, language universals are more commonly associated with the study of language and mind. This is the topic of the next chapter.

Questions

1 What problems arise in an attempt to define the notion of a 'language'?
2 Distinguish between **dialect** and **accent**.
3 Which socio-economic class is likely to show the greatest phonological variation within its speech, and why?
4 In what ways might women's speech differ from men's?
5 What is **language planning**, and how might it be carried out effectively?
6 What is a **pidgin**, and how may it be distinguished from a **creole**?

language and mind

This chapter looks at psycholinguistics, and outlines three core areas: how humans acquire language, how they comprehend speech, and how they produce it. It also looks briefly at speech disorders, and where language might be located in the brain.

Psycholinguistics is often defined as the study of language and the mind. It explores what goes on in the human mind as an individual acquires, comprehends, produces and stores language. Such a study covers an enormous range of topics, and no two psycholinguists agree on exactly the ground which it covers. One reason for this disagreement is that psycholinguistics overlaps with a somewhat wider study, sometimes called the **psychology of communication**, which looks at language alongside other human methods of communication, such as the use of gesture and facial expressions.

This chapter outlines some of the work going on in three 'core' psycholinguistic topics:

How humans acquire language.
How humans comprehend speech.
How humans produce speech.

It also discusses how the study of language and mind overlaps with that of language and the brain.

Psycholinguistic evidence

The mind cannot be directly observed, so psycholinguists have to devise ways of finding out how it works. They get their evidence from two main sources: observation of spontaneous utterances, on the one hand, and psycholinguistic experiments, on the other.

Spontaneous utterances which deviate from the norm in some way are the most informative. We can learn considerably more from a child's mistake such as *foots* instead of 'feet', or someone who said *geranium* instead of 'hydrangea', than we can from a perfect flow of speech.

However, ordinary speech is somewhat messy, in that there are dozens of different factors which have to be taken into account when utterances are analyzed. Psycholinguists therefore devise experiments in which the number of variable factors can be controlled, and the results can be accurately measured. They might, for example, set subjects a 'lexical decision task', in which they time how long it takes a person to recognize a word as being a word, or reject a nonsense sequence such as *vleesidence* as a non-word.

But this type of methodology presents a problem, sometimes called the 'experimental paradox'. The more carefully an experiment is devised so as to limit variables, the more subjects are put into an unnatural situation, in which they are likely to behave oddly. On the other hand, the more one allows a situation to be like 'real-life', the less one is able to sort out the various interacting factors.

Ideally, major topics should be tackled both by observing spontaneous speech and by devising experiments. And when the results coincide, this is a sign that progress is being made.

Acquiring language

The so-called 'innateness question' has been a burning issue over the last half century. Exactly how much language is pre-programmed within the human mind? Do humans have a genetically imprinted 'Universal Grammar', as Chomsky suggests? Or were the rudiments of language invented by a clever cave-man and handed down from generation to generation? No detailed solution has yet been found to these questions. But by examining them, we are slowly acquiring a greater understanding of the nature of human language.

One point in particular has become clearer: language has all the hallmarks of **maturationally controlled behaviour**. It used to be thought that animal behaviour could be divided into two types: that which was inborn and natural (for example, dogs naturally bark), and that which was learned and unnatural (dogs may be taught to beg). It turns out, however, that this division is by no means clearcut and may be misleading. Many types of behaviour develop 'naturally' at a certain age, provided that the surrounding environment is adequate. Such behaviour is maturationally controlled, and sexual activity is a typical example. Arguments as to whether it is inborn or learnt are futile. Both nature and nurture are important. Innate potentialities lay down the framework, and within this framework, there is wide variation depending on the environment. When individuals reach a crucial point in their maturation, they are biologically in a state of readiness for learning the behaviour. They would not learn it at this time without a biological trigger and, conversely, the biological trigger could not be activated if there was nobody around from whom they could learn the behaviour.

Human infants pay attention to language from birth. They produce recognizable words at around 12–15 months, and start putting words together at around 18 months. The urge for language to emerge at this time is very strong, and only very extraordinary circumstances will suppress it – as in the case of Genie, a Californian teenager who from the age of 20 months had been confined to one small room, and had been physically punished by her father if she made any sounds. Naturally, she was without speech when she was found.

But all normal children, and some abnormal ones, will begin to speak if they hear language going on around them. Take Laura, a severely retarded girl who produced fluent and richly structured speech, as:

He was saying that I lost my battery-powered watch that I loved.

She was not just parroting sentences she had heard, because she made some grammatical errors, as:

Three tickets were gave out by a police last year.

This linguistic fluency contrasted strongly with her inability to handle other everyday matters: she did not even know her age!

The content–process controversy

The realization that language is maturationally controlled means that most psycholinguists now agree that human beings are innately programmed to speak. But they cannot agree on exactly *what* is innate. In particular, they cannot decide to what extent (if any) language ability is separate from other cognitive abilities.

All researchers agree that there is extraordinary similarity in the speech development of English-speaking children. Children who could not possibly be acquainted go through similar stages in their development, and also make similar mistakes. The implications of this coincidence are hotly disputed. On the one hand, there are those who consider that this uniformity of speech development indicates that children innately *contain* a blueprint for language: this view represents a so-called **content** approach. Extreme supporters of this view suggest that children may have a universal framework imprinted on their brains.

On the other hand, there are those who support a **process** approach, and argue that children could not possibly contain specific language universals. Instead, they are innately geared to *processing* linguistic data, for which they utilize a puzzle-solving ability which is closely related to other cognitive skills.

A further group of people point to the social nature of language, and the role of parents. Children, they argue, are social beings who have a great need to interact with those around them. Furthermore, all over the world, child-carers tend to talk about the same sort of things, chatting mainly about food, clothes and other objects in the immediate environment. **Motherese** or **caregiver language** has fairly similar characteristics almost everywhere: the caregivers slow down their rate of speech, and speak in slow, well-formed utterances, with quite a lot of repetition. People who stress these social aspects of language claim that there is no need to search for complex innate mechanisms: social interaction with caring caregivers is sufficient to cause language to develop.

This latter view is turning out to be something of an exaggeration. The fact that parents make it easier for children to learn language does not explain why they are so quick to acquire it: intelligent chimps exposed to intensive sign language rarely get beyond 200 words and two-word sentences. Furthermore, language seems to be due to something more than a desire to communicate. There is at least one strange child on record who acquired fluent language, but did not use it to communicate. He spoke only monologues to himself, and refused to interact with others.

The whole controversy is far from solved. But increasingly, language is thought to be **innately guided behaviour** (Chapter 2). Humans are naturally 'tuned in' to language. They instinctively pick out speech sounds, and know how to build them into linguistic grammars.

The rule-governed nature of child language

In spite of the numerous controversies surrounding child language, psycholinguists are at least in agreement on one major point. Children are not simply imitating what they hear going on around them as if they were parrots. The learning processes involved are far more complex. From the moment they begin to talk, children seem to be aware that language is **rule-governed**, and they are engaged in an active search for the rules which underlie the language to which they are exposed. Child language is never at any time a haphazard conglomeration of random words, or a sub-standard version of adult speech. Instead, every child at every stage possesses a grammar with rules of its own even though the system will be simpler than that of an adult. For example, when children first use negatives, they normally use a simple rule: 'Put *no* or *not* in front of the sentence.' This results in consistent negative sentences which the child could not possibly have heard from an adult:

No play that.
No Fraser drink all tea.

This rule is generally superseded by another which says: 'Insert the negative after the first NP.' This also produces a consistent set of sentences which the child is unlikely to have heard from an adult:

*Doggie **no** bite.*
*That **no** mummy.*

A rather more obvious example of the rule-governed nature of child language are forms such as *mans*, *foots*, *gooses*, which children produce frequently. Such plurals occur even when a child understands and responds correctly to the adult forms *men*, *feet*, *geese*. This is clear proof that children's own rules of grammar are more important to them than mere imitation.

Children do not, however, formulate a new rule overnight, and suddenly replace the old one with this new one. Instead, there is considerable fluctuation between the old and the new. The new construction appears at first in a limited number of places. A child might first use the word *what* in a phrase with a single verb:

***What** mummy doing?*
***What** daddy doing?*
***What** Billy doing?*

then only gradually extend it to other verbs, as in:

***What** kitty eating?*
***What** mummy sewing?*

This process is somewhat like the way in which an alteration creeps from word to word in language change (Chapter 13).

Attention to the ways in which children move from one rule to another has shown that language acquisition is not as uniform as was once thought. Different children use different strategies for acquiring speech. For example, some seem to concentrate on the overall rhythm, and slot in words with the same general sound pattern, whereas others prefer to deal with more abstract slots. Of particular interest is work which looks at how children cope with different languages. This enables researchers to see if children have any universal expectations about how language behaves, or whether they wait and see what their own particular language offers.

Some recent work has tried to simulate on a computer how children learn past tenses, with some success. First the computer, like children, learned irregular past tenses correctly, such as *caught*, *went*. Then, as children do, it overregularized them, and produced forms such as *catched*, *goed*. Eventually, like children, it successfully handled the past tenses of almost all the verbs fed into it. But two opposite conclusions have been drawn from this: either language is straightforward, if it can be handled by a well-programmed computer. Or, word endings are a small, and not very difficult part of language. Time will tell if computers can be programmed to acquire more complex aspects of language.

Learning the meaning of words

Children have to learn not only the syntax and sounds of their language, but also the meaning of words. This turns out to be more complicated than some people suppose. For a start, it probably takes some time for children to discover that words can refer to separate things. At first, they probably think that a word such as *milk* refers to a whole generalized ritual, something uttered as a mug is placed in front of them. Later, they discover that words have meanings which can be applied to individual objects and actions.

At first, children may be able to use words only in a particular context. One child agreed that *snow* was white, but refused to accept that a piece of paper was also white. This tendency to **undergeneralize** usually passes unnoticed. But it is probably commoner than **overgeneralization**, which attracts much more attention.

People often remark on children's overgeneralizations. Youngsters may call any type of small thing a *crumb*: a crumb, a small beetle, or a speck of dirt, or they may apply the word *moon* to any kind of light. An idea popular in the 19th century was that children see the world through a mental fog. They are able only to grasp broad outlines, which they then narrow down.

But this turns out to be an oversimplification, because children's overgeneralizations are often quite specific, and quite odd. One child referred to a shiny green leaf as a moon! A possible explanation is that she was working from a prototype (Chapter 8) which was unlike the adult's prototype. This child had apparently taken a picture of a shiny yellow crescent moon as a prototypical moon, and re-applied the word *moon* to anything which had the approximate shape of the original, as well as one of its other characteristics. The leaf was vaguely crescent shaped, and also shiny. This interesting idea is currently being explored by researchers.

Doing it by hand

The urge to communicate is strong in humans, and those who cannot hear can be taught sign language. Sign language is a full language in every way, but it is important for children to start acquiring it young. Deaf children with deaf parents start signing earlier, and quickly become more proficient than deaf children with hearing parents.

In Nicaragua, a community of deaf youngsters has invented its own sign language. At first, the youngsters learned a general hotch-potch of different signs from others around. But by around 20 years later, they had developed these signs into a full language. These Nicaraguan signers show how strong the urge is for language to emerge, and how quickly young humans can devise a language system: all they need is a few signs to get them going, and a group of people who interact using them.

Recognizing words

Understanding speech is not the simple matter it appears to be at first sight. Most people assume that comprehension involves being a passive recipient of someone else's message. Hearers, it is often supposed, behave like secretaries taking down a mental dictation. They mentally record the message, then read it back to themselves.

This assumption turns out to be quite wrong. For a start, it is physically impossible to recognize each separate sound, speech is just too fast. Understanding language is an *active*, not a passive process. Hearers jump to conclusions on the basis of partial information. This has been demonstrated in various experiments. For example, listeners were asked to interpret the following sentences, in which the first sound of the final word was indistinct.

Paint the fence and the ?ate.
Check the calendar and the ?ate.
Here's the fishing gear and the ?ate.

The subjects claimed to hear *gate* in the first sentence, *date* in the second, and *bait* in the third.

Since recognizing words involves quite a lot of guesswork, how do speakers make the guesses? Suppose someone had heard 'She saw a do–'. Would the hearer check through the possible candidates one after the other, *dog, doll, don, dock*, and so on (**serial** processing)? Or would all the possibilities be considered subconsciously at the same time (**parallel** processing)?

The human mind, it appears, prefers the second method, that of parallel processing, so much so that even unlikely possibilities are probably considered subconsciously. A recent **interactive activation** theory suggests that the mind is an enormously powerful network in which any word which at all resembles the one heard is automatically activated, and that each of these triggers its own neighbours, so that activation gradually spreads like ripples on a pond. Words that seem particularly appropriate get more and more excited, and those which are irrelevant gradually fade away. Eventually, one candidate wins out over the others.

Understanding syntax

We now know quite a lot about word recognition. But it is still unclear how separate words are woven together into the overall pattern.

To some extent, the process is similar to word recognition, in that people look for outline clues, and then actively reconstruct the probable message from them. In linguistic terminology, hearers utilize **perceptual strategies**. They jump to conclusions on the basis of outline clues by imposing what they expect to hear onto the stream of sounds. For example, consider the sentence:

The boy kicked the ball threw it back.

Most people who hear this sentence feel that there is something wrong with it, that there is a word left out somewhere, and that it would preferably be:

*The boy **who** kicked the ball threw it back.*
*The boy kicked the ball, **then** threw it back.*

However, they realize that it is in fact perfectly well-formed when shown a similar sentence:

The boy thrown the ball kicked it back. (The boy to whom the ball was thrown kicked it back.)

The problem arose because when interpreting sentences, people tend to impose a subject-verb-object sequence on them. It is hard to counteract this tendency, and accounts for a number of **garden-path** sentences, situations in which hearers are initially led 'up the garden path' in their interpretation, before realizing they have made a mistake, as in:

Anyone who cooks ducks out of the washing-up. (Anyone who cooks tries to avoid or ducks out of the washing-up.)

In other cases, however, people's interpretation varies depending on the lexical items. In:

Clever girls and boys go to university,

people usually assume that *clever* refers both to girls and boys. But in:

Small dogs and cats do not need much exercise,

small is usually taken to refer to the dogs alone.

The relationship between lexical items, the syntax, and the overall context therefore is still under discussion. A further problem is that of **gaps**, situations in which a word has been brought to the front of the sentence, and left a 'gap' after the verb, as in:

Which wombat did Bill put in the cage?

Do hearers mentally store *which wombat* until they find the place in the sentence which it slots into (in this case, after the verb *put*)? Or what happens? This matter is still hotly disputed.

Speech production

Speech production involves at least two types of process. On the one hand, words have to be selected. On the other, they have to be integrated into the syntax.

Slips of the tongue – cases in which the speaker accidentally says something such as *par cark* instead of 'car park' – provide useful clues to these processes, and so do pauses: they can tell us where a speaker stops to think – though it is difficult to separate out pauses caused by searching for lexical items, and pauses due to syntactic planning.

There are two main kinds of slips: on the one hand, there are **selection errors,** cases in which a speaker has picked out the wrong item, as in:

*Please hand me the **tin-opener*** (nut-crackers).

*Your seat's in the third **component*** (compartment).

On the other hand, there are **assemblage errors,** cases in which a correct choice has been made, but the utterance has been wrongly assembled:

Dinner** is being served at **wine (Wine is being served at dinner).

*A **poppy** of my **caper*** (A copy of my paper).

At first sight, such slips may seem haphazard and confused. On closer inspection, they show certain regularities, so much so that some people have talked about tongue slip 'laws' – though this is something of an exaggeration. We are dealing with recurring probabilities, rather than any real kind of 'law'.

Selection errors usually involve lexical items, so they can tell us which words are closely associated in the mind. For example, people tend to say *knives* for 'forks', *oranges* for 'lemons', *left* for 'right', suggesting that words on the same general level of detail are tightly linked, especially if they are thought of as a pair. Similar sounding words which get confused tend to have similar beginnings and endings, and a similar rhythm, as in *antidote* for 'anecdote', *confusion* for 'conclusion'.

These observations were possibly first made by the two Harvard psychologists who devised a now famous 'tip of the tongue' experiment. The experimenters assembled a number of students, and read them out definitions of relatively uncommon words. For example, 'A navigational instrument used in measuring angular distances, especially the altitude of sun, moon and stars at sea'. Some of the students were unable to write down the word *sextant* immediately. The word was on the tip of their tongue, but they could not quite remember it. Those in a 'tip of the tongue state' were asked to fill in a questionnaire about their mental search. They found that they could provide quite a lot of information about the elusive word. They could often say how many syllables it had, what the first letter was, and sometimes, how it ended. They could think up similar-meaning words such as *astrolabe*, *compass*, and also similar-sounding words such as *secant*, *sexton*, *sextet*. This suggests that adults store and select words partly on the basis of rhythm, partly by remembering how they begin and end.

A considerable number of selection errors tend to be similar both in sound and meaning, as in *component* for 'compartment', *geraniums* for 'hydrangeas'. This suggests that an interactive activation theory, of the type proposed for speech recognition, may also be relevant in speech production. The mind activates all similar words, and those that have two kinds of similarity, both meaning and sound, get more highly activated than the others, and so are more likely to pop up in error.

Whereas selection errors tell us how individual words are stored and selected, assemblage errors indicate how whole sequences are organized ready for production. For example, mistakes nearly always take place within a single 'tone-group' – a short stretch of speech spoken with a single intonation contour. This suggests that the tone group is the unit of planning. And within the tone group, items with similar stress are often transposed, as in:

A gas of tank (a tank of gas).

Furthermore, when sounds are switched, initial sounds change place with other initials, and final with final, and so on, as in:

Reap of hubbish (heap of rubbish).
Hass or grash (hash or grass).

All this suggests that speech is organized in accordance with a rhythmic principle – that a tone group is divided into smaller units (usually called feet), which are based (in English) on stress. Feet are divided into syllables, which are in turn possibly controlled by a biological 'beat' which regulates the speed of utterance. The interaction between these rhythmically based tone groups and syntactic constructions is a topic which still needs to be carefully examined.

Slips of the tongue are part of *normal* speech. Everybody makes them. But they overlap with the stranger and more extreme errors found in people suffering from speech disorders.

Speech disorders

'Lovely rabbit' said a woman who had had a stroke, when shown a picture of an apple. By chance, she had been talking about rhubarb previously, and so had somehow blended the words *apple* and *rhubarb* into *rabbit*. She was suffering from **aphasia**, the general word for serious speech disorders, which literally means 'without speech'. In fact, such speakers usually have some speech, but speech of a rather odd kind. It's important to distinguish them from those who simply have a problem in 'spitting out' what they want to say, such as stutterers.

Aphasic patients are difficult to classify, because damage to the brain is hardly ever neat and tidy. The tissues may swell, some areas are likely to be starved of blood and oxygen, and the brain often tries to compensate in unpredictable ways. So every patient's symptoms are slightly different – though almost all of them have problems in finding words, a problem known as **anomia**, literally 'without naming ability'.

But it is sometimes possible to classify disorders into broad types. On the one hand, there are people who have huge difficulty in stringing words together into sentences. They speak effortfully, typically in three or four word bursts, using nouns above all. There are hardly any endings on words, and the 'little words', such as *a*, *the*, *on*, *to*, are likely to be missing. One patient, when asked if he went home from hospital at weekends, replied: 'Why, yes ... Thursday, er, er, er, no, er, Friday... Barbara wife ... and, oh, car ... drive ...'. **Agrammatism** is the technical name for this man's condition, because his speech appears to be without grammar – though he can mostly understand other people quite well, and answer appropriately.

In contrast, others suffer from **fluent aphasia**. As the name suggests, these patients speak fluently, though they tend not to make sense. They also produce strange made-up words, and often have severe problems comprehending what is said to them. One patient, when asked why he was in hospital, produced a stream of meaningless gibberish: 'I can't mention the tarripoi ... I impose a lot, while, on the other hand, you know what I mean, I have to run around, look it over, trebbin, and all that sort of stuff.'

These two broad varieties of disorder are not the only ones, but they are possibly the commonest, with agrammatism being more frequently found than fluent aphasia. From them (and other sources), linguists try to draw conclusions about how humans organize language. For example, fluent aphasics suggest that speech production and speech comprehension might be to a large extent separate, since one can exist without the other.

The study of aphasia, technically **aphasiology**, represents the borderline between the mind and the brain. Psycholinguistics 'proper' tries to map out what is happening in the mind, independently of how language is organized in the brain. Just as one could study the bus routes in London, without knowing anything about the physical nature of buses, so one could find out quite a lot about how language works without worrying about the neurons which allow this to happen. But as knowledge about the brain improves, psycholinguistics increasingly incorporates knowledge about the brain, technically **neurolinguistics**. And a question which has been discussed for well over a century is whether particular types of language disorder can be correlated with damage to particular areas within the brain.

Language and the brain

The human brain is roughly organized like a peach, in that there is a large outer layer (the **cerebrum**) surrounding an inner kernel (the **brainstem**), which keeps people alive. The outer layer is extensively folded, and is the source of all intentional thought and movement. After death, it is grey, as reflected in the phrase: 'Use your grey matter' for 'Think!', and is divided into two halves, the **cerebral hemispheres**. The left hemisphere controls the right side of the body, and the right hemisphere the left: so if someone is paralyzed down the right side of their body after a stroke, the stroke affected the left side of their brain.

The hemispheres look roughly similar, but this is an illusion. One of them, usually the left, is the more powerful **dominant** hemisphere. This is not only because it controls the right side of the body – and the majority of humans are right-handed – but also because it normally controls language. Approximately 90 per cent of the human race are born with their brain 'wired' for language in the left hemisphere. Humans who do not have language in their left hemisphere are often, though not inevitably, left-handers. This much is fairly uncontroversial.

But disputes begin when attempts are made to locate language precisely within the left hemisphere. Once again, the outline is clearer than the details. Those who have problems with speech production, such as agrammatic aphasics, mostly have injuries towards the front of the brain, while those who have problems with comprehension, such as fluent aphasics, have injuries towards the back.

These disputes began in the 19th century, when Paul Broca, a French surgeon, pinpointed an area in front of, and slightly above, the left ear. According to him, postmortems showed that this area had been destroyed in the brain of two patients who could produce hardly any speech. Even today, damage to the general region known as **Broca's area** is statistically likely to cause severe speech problems – so much so that agrammatic speech is still sometimes known as **Broca's aphasia** (Figure 11.1).

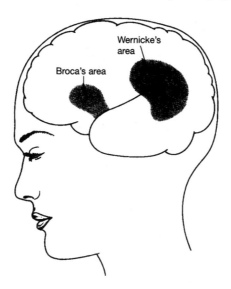

figure 11.1

Some years after Broca's claims, Karl Wernicke, a German neurologist, noted that several patients who talked fluent nonsense had severe damage towards the back of the brain, in an area under and surrounding the left ear. This became known as **Wernicke's area,** and fluent aphasics are sometimes said to be suffering from **Wernicke's aphasia** (Figure 11.1).

But brain areas cannot be as accurately located as the heart or liver. So over the years, patients have been found who can speak perfectly well, even though Broca's region has been damaged, as well as people who cannot speak when Broca's area is apparently intact. Some neurolinguists argue that speech is therefore located slightly differently in each person, while others claim that connections within the brain matter more than specific areas.

Brain scans are beginning to supplement our information. Whenever anyone uses language, blood surges through the brain. This blood flow can be seen and measured by injecting radioactive water into the blood stream. Different brain areas become active in different linguistic tasks. Choosing a verb has turned out to be a complex process, in which several different areas are involved. In addition, a regular past tense such as *climbed* shows a different blood flow pattern from an irregular one, such as *caught*. This is currently an important area of research.

This chapter has looked at how humans acquire, comprehend and produce speech. It has also considered briefly how the study of language and mind overlaps with that of language and the brain. Recent advances in both areas suggest that in the future, the link-up may become closer.

Questions

1 What is meant by **maturationally controlled behaviour**?
2 What is the **content–process** controversy?
3 Child language is **rule-governed**. Explain this statement.
4 What are **perceptual strategies**?
5 How might a psycholinguist find out about sentence production?
6 Outline the main symptoms of two types of **aphasia**.

12

language and style

This chapter looks at literary language, and discusses where it overlaps with, and where it differs from 'ordinary' language. It also discusses the language of advertising and newspaper language.

'Philosophy will clip an angel's wings', according to the 19th-century poet, John Keats. Likewise, many have been unwilling to dissect literature, fearing analysis would destroy its magic.

But literary language is not a bizarre confection of angel-dust. Instead, it overlaps strongly with various other types of language, including everyday language. At one time, literature was thought to break linguistic 'rules'. Nowadays, the belief that 'real' rules can be firmly specified and divided from 'broken' rules has faded: language is flexible and fuzzy-edged.

In addition, the label 'literature' has been re-assessed. Literature is 'highly valued writing', and non-literature is 'lowly valued writing' – just as a flower is a desired plant, and a weed an unwanted one. The judgement varies, depending on the judge: values alter from generation to generation. What is prized in one century may be condemned in the next. And at all times, 'good' literature merges into 'bad', with no firm divide-line.

This chapter looks at literary language, and explores where it overlaps with, and where it differs from 'ordinary' language. It also discusses two other related types of specialized language, newspaper language and advertising language.

Style and stylistics

The linguistic analysis of literary language is known as **stylistics**. This is a somewhat misleading term: the word 'styles' was once applied to different varieties of language, such as the language of religion, or of legal documents. But these varieties are now often known as **registers** (Chapter 10). Meanwhile, the words **style** and **stylistics** have acquired the somewhat specialized, narrow usage of linguistics applied to literature.

Literary language often deviates from everyday language, even though it is in no way deviant. Typically, certain features have been highlighted, or **foregrounded**, often by making them strange. Foregrounding has two intertwined meanings. On the one hand, it involves bringing forward literary usages against the background of expectations about ordinary usage. On the other hand, certain features are made prominent or foregrounded within a text. As the term **foregrounding** suggests, literary language is intentionally compared with the visual arts, where an artist is likely to emphasize some aspects of a painting over others.

A poem about the wind is likely to differ from, say, a chat about the weather. But poetry cannot be too peculiar, or readers and listeners would simply 'turn off'. Only a small and predictable proportion of language can be varied. Let us consider this further.

The same bright, patient stars

'And still they were the same bright, patient stars', said Keats in his poem *Hyperion*. And in literary language the phonology, morphology and (mostly) the syntax are the same bright, patient stars. They may sometimes deviate from the norm, but do so relatively little.

Take phonology. 'Be wery careful o' vidders [widows] all your life', says Mr Weller in Charles Dickens' *Pickwick Papers*, his cockney accent signalled primarily by the switch of *v* and *w*. Non-standard accents are usually represented, as here, via only occasional changes to the normal spelling.

Inflectional morphemes – meaningful chunks of words which alter the relation of a word to the rest of the sentence (Chapter 6) – are rarely altered, except in comic verse:

> *Tell me, o octopus, I **begs**,*
> *Is those things arms, or is they legs?*

Ogden Nash

Syntax may deviate more than morphology, though any deviation is likely to be minor, as:

> ***About the woodlands*** *I will go*
> *To see the cherry hung with snow*
> A. E. Housman

> *And like a dying lady, **lean and pale**,*
> *Who totters forth, wrapped in a gauzy veil,*
> Percy Bysshe Shelley

> *I see a lily on thy brow,*
> *With anguish **moist** and fever dew;*
> John Keats

In these examples, the syntactic variation is trivial: the bold phrases and words would be in only a slightly different position in ordinary conversation: 'I will go about the woodlands', 'Like a lean and pale dying lady', 'moist with anguish and fever dew'.

Major contortions are rarely found, they would disrupt comprehension too much.

Ways with words

Words are the wool out of which literature is knitted. Yet these are mainly existing ones, used in novel ways: brand new words are relatively rare in serious writing.

A bunch of oldish words are sometimes thought of as poetic, such as *quoth*, *fain*, *behold*, as also are some conventional abbreviations: *o'er*, *'twas*, *ne'er*. Yet these have always been sparsely used, and most are now unusual even in literature.

Writers are like knitters trying to invent new patterns. They avoid obvious sequences such as *black despair*, *green fingers* or *purple patch*, and devise new, original combinations. 'And then the lover,/ Sighing like a furnace …', said Shakespeare; 'Birds the colour of red-flannel petticoats whisked past the harp-shaped hills', described Dylan Thomas of his childhood. A thrush sings, with 'Its fresh-peeled voice/ Astonishing the brickwork', wrote the poet Philip Larkin.

These examples contain so-called **tropes**, an old technical term from rhetoric for 'figures of speech' which involve meaning. These are traditionally connected with poetic meaning. Let us consider the main ones further.

Twisting words

The name *trope* comes originally from the Greek word for twisting or turning. **Simile** is possibly the most straightforward. It involves an explicit comparison of two unlike things, as in 'Fame is like a river' (Francis Bacon).

Metaphor is perhaps the best known trope, once defined by the Greek philosopher Aristotle as 'the application to one thing of a name belonging to another'. For example, 'Fame is a food' ('Fame is a food that dead men eat', once said by the poet Austin Dobson), when fame is clearly *not* something which can be literally devoured.

Metaphor is sometimes assumed to be fundamentally poetic in nature. And poetry does indeed teem with metaphor. But so does everyday speech. Metaphor is an inevitable part of day-to-day language, as in:

*Pauline's a **gold-digger**.*
*Felix tried to **get his ideas across**.*
*Marigold **shot down** his arguments.*
*That marriage is **dead**.*
*Students shouldn't be **spoon-fed**.*
*Henry is **fighting a grim battle** with illness.*

And so on, and so on. It is impossible to do without it, especially in areas where drama is low, such as finance:

*The dollar **tumbled** to a new low.*
*Will our **bubble economy go pop**?*

Yet many everyday metaphors are stale: clichés such as *black mood*, *white lie* are sometimes even labelled 'dead metaphors'. Poetic metaphors are fresh. And more often than in ordinary conversation, they conjure up a whole novel scene, as in Shakespeare's famous line:

Sleep, which knits up the ravelled sleeve of care.

Here *sleep* does not relate to only one word, instead a whole knitting scenario is envisaged.

Quality rather than quantity, then, is what distinguishes poetic metaphors from everyday ones: the best are both novel and appropriate. They surprise the reader, but do not seem bizarre.

Gluing it all together

The moan of doves in immemorial elms,
And murmuring of innumerable bees.

Lord Alfred Tennyson

These lines of Tennyson are often quoted as an instance of 'poetic' writing. They attempt to reproduce the sound of doves cooing and bees humming, technically, **onomatopoeia**. This drowsy hum effect has been created above all by **repetition**, in this case mainly of the sounds *m* and *r*.

Repetition is a glue which helps a work of literature to hang together as a whole, or **cohere**. Of course, real life conversation is enormously repetitious, as: 'Football, football, everybody keeps talking about football'. The planned and patterned nature of literary repetition is what distinguishes it from everyday repeats.

Rhyme and **metre** are types of repetition strongly associated with poetry. In rhyme, the ends of words are repeated, as:

> *That orbèd **maiden** with white fire **laden,***
> *Whom mortals call the **Moon,***
> *Glides glimmering o'er my fleece-like **floor,***
> *By the midnight breezes **strewn.***

Percy Bysshe Shelley

Poetic metre may at first sight seem artificial, with recurring types of *foot* (unit of rhythm). Yet poetry does not use bizarre, invented beats. Instead, it is ultimately based on spoken language. Large chunks of it are written in the *dum-di dum-di* 'Monday, Tuesday ...', 'bread 'n butter' pattern widely found in everyday speech, as in:

> *Tyger! Tyger! burning bright*
> *In the forests of the night ...*

William Blake

– though various other metres are found, some quite complex ones.

Poetic metres differ from spoken speech rhythms primarily in that they are more repetitious, and more consistent, even though an intentional sudden breaking of the metrical pattern can create a special effect, as when a boat rushing over the waves (*dum-di, dum-di, dum-di*) suddenly thumps up against them (*dum, dum, dum*):

> *Dirty British coaster with a salt-caked smoke stack*
> *Butting through the channel in the mad March days ...*

John Masefield

Saying it again, but subtly

> *By the shores of Gitche Gumee*
> *By the shining Big-Sea-Water,*
> *Stood the wigwam of Nokomis,*
> *Daughter of the Moon, Nokomis ...*
> Henry W. Longfellow

These lines from 'Hiawatha' contain obvious repetition. Yet much of literature hangs together via less obvious repetitious devices. 'Hiawatha' continues:

> *Dark behind it rose the forest,*
> *Rose the black and gloomy pine-trees,*
> *Rose the firs with cones upon them ...*

Firs and pines are both types of trees, and a collection of trees makes up a forest. The poet assumes that the readers know all this. Or:

> They shut the road through the woods
> Seventy years ago.
> Weather and rain have undone it again,
> And now you would never know
> There was once a path through the woods
> Before they planted the trees.

Rudyard Kipling

These lines seem straightforward, yet closely-connected words help to link them together, as *road* and *path*, *trees* and *woods*, *rain* and *weather*.

Yet repetition, or near-repetition, plays only a partial role. Above all, successful literary works have an underlying structure – and so do many other forms of language, as will be outlined below.

Searching for the skeleton: poems, news

Words are like the flesh on an underlying skeleton. The bones vary in their rigidity. Some verse is tightly formed: sonnets have a fourteen-line structure, and limericks a five-line one, as:

> There was an Old Man of the coast,
> Who placidly sat on a post;
> But when it was cold,
> He relinquished his hold,
> And called for some hot buttered toast.

Edward Lear

Other written forms have a less obvious structure. Take newspaper reports. It is fashionable to moan about 'journalese'. Yet this is unwarranted. The vocabulary and style are straightforward: trainee journalists are advised to follow the 'rules' of clear writing proposed by the writer George Orwell, which include:

Never use a long word where a short one will do.
If it is possible to cut out a word, always cut it out.
Never use a passive where you can use an active.

And so on.

What *is* complex is the structure underlying the news stories. New information is placed first within a *what-where-(when)-who-how-(why)* summary, a so-called 'hard news' formula whose purpose is to orient the reader fast as to *what* happened, *where* it happened, *who* was involved, *how* it occurred, and *why* it happened – though *when* is often missing, because news is assumed to be new and recent, and *why* is not always known. For example:

> At least 26 people were killed and more than 200 injured when a huge car bomb ripped through the centre of Omagh, County Tyrone, yesterday afternoon.

A huge amount of important information is tightly packed into that first sentence, which provides a concise account of the whole event – a summary that only skilled journalists can easily write, and the headline is commonly written from that summary.

After the summary, the story consists of a sequence of events, though not necessarily in order of occurrence: the most recent come first. A high level of skill is required to present this information clearly, and in an interesting fashion. Eventually comes a final sentence outlining the current 'state of play' – though this must never contain crucial information, because it is likely to be cut if space is short (Figure 12.1).

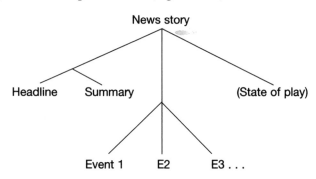

figure 12.1

The language of advertising

Musk. The missing link between animal and man. Earthy, Primitive. Fiercely masculine. (cosmetic advertisement)

*Outspan. The great taste of grapefruit. Cool, refreshing, full
of flavour. Wholesome, natural grapefruit – the colour of the
sun. Puts the rest in the shade.* (fruit advertisement)

Advertising copywriters, like journalists, have to present their
message briefly, and in an eye-catching way.

There are three major ways in which advertisers get their effect.
They write it large, they make it short, they make it 'jingly'. The
magazine advertisements quoted above were printed in larger
than usual print, so it was hard not to read them as one flipped
through the pages, just as it is hard not to read billboards on the
roadside.

Words that are inessential for the meaning are omitted, so most of
the 'sentences' do not contain a verb. Consider how
comparatively dull the result would have been with verbs: 'Think
about musk. It is the missing link between animal and man. It is
earthy. It is primitive. It is fiercely masculine.' If verbs are used in
the main message of an advertisement, they are often imperatives:

Drinka pinta milka day.
Go to work on an egg.
Have a break, have a Kitkat.

If they are not imperatives, they are almost always in the present
tense, and negatives are rare:

Persil washes whiter.
Oxo gives a meal man appeal.
You can take a White Horse anywhere.

In an extended advertisement, the wording often follows a
formula. First, the 'key' word, followed by a longer sequence:
'Musk. The missing link between animal and man.' Then
comes a series of shortish, catchy phrases. Important words
are backed up with near-synonyms: 'Earthy. Primitive'; 'Cool,
refreshing'; 'Wholesome, natural'. There's likely to be a pun
somewhere: 'The colour of the sun – puts the rest in the shade'.
It's easy to think up other examples of plays on words in well-
known ads:

Better in jams than strawberries. (car advertisement)
Players please. (cigarette advertisement)

These strategies are not only used to make people buy particular
shampoos or perfumes. They are also utilized by politicians, as
in the slogans of political parties:

Let's go with Labour. (Labour party slogan)
Labour isn't working. (Conservative party slogan)

But not all 'advertising' is so straightforward. Less obvious, and so more dangerous, are some of the other techniques used by politicians, such as the use of metaphor. Subtle and skilful use of metaphor can influence people's thoughts in a way in which they are unaware. The *arms race* is a classic example. Politicians sometimes pretend that their nation is in an athletic contest with other nations, even though this may be entirely in their imagination. Richard Nixon, an ex-president of America, repeatedly emphasized how important it was to 'win' in the 'race' against other countries: 'This nation cannot stand still because we are in a deadly competition ... We're ahead in this competition ... but when you're in a race the only way to stay ahead is to move ahead'.

These days, nuclear weapons attract a high number of metaphors. These hideously dangerous devices tend to be referred to by politicians as 'nuclear shields' or 'nuclear deterrents', or a 'nuclear umbrella'. This leads people to believe that they are genuinely necessary (we all need umbrellas), purely defensive (shields), and even useful in discouraging others from warfare (deterrents). These beliefs may, or may not, be true. But the language used in discussing nuclear armaments ensures that the average person does not look beyond the reassuring language, and therefore fails to perceive the potential dangers involved. In an ideal world, everyone would be able to recognize linguistic manipulation, and question whether it was conveying or hiding the truth.

This chapter, then, has pointed out some of the ways in which skilled word weavers – especially poets, journalists and advertising copywriters – get their effect, and how they may manipulate the unwary.

Questions

1 What is **foregrounding**?
2 Which part of language is most often creatively extended by poets?
3 How does literary metaphor differ from metaphor in day-to-day language?
4 Outline three types of **repetition** found in poetry, and suggest why repetition is so widespread.
5 What is the '**hard news**' formula, and what is its purpose?
6 Outline some strategies used by advertisers.

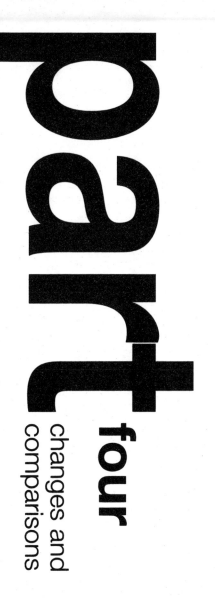

part four

changes and comparisons

Change and decay in all around we see. But not all change is decay, and some decay turns into new life.

D.J. Enright

13

language
change

This chapter considers how
and why language changes. It
also lists the main methods
used to reconstruct past
stages of languages for which
written records are sparse or
unavailable.

All languages are continually changing – their sounds, their syntax and their meaning. This gradual alteration is mostly unnoticed by the speakers of a language, since the sounds and syntax in particular give a superficial impression of being static. Yet one glance at the works of Chaucer or Shakespeare shows how much English has changed in a relatively short time.

A closer look at the English of today reveals several sounds and constructions in the process of changing. [j], the *y*-like sound which occurs before [uː] in words such as *tune, muse, duty,* seems to be dropping out. It has already disappeared in words such as *rule, lute.* Soon, it may have dropped out entirely, as it has in the East Anglian region of England.

Meanwhile, a change in syntax is occurring in the use of the pronouns *I* and *me.* It used to be considered correct to say *It's I.* Nowadays, the majority of people say *It's me. Me* tends to be used after the verb, and *I* before it. And there are signs that this rule is being extended so that *I* occurs only in a position directly preceding the verb. The line in the popular song, 'Me and the elephant, we still remember you', is only partially a joke. Such sentences possibly encapsulate this changing rule of grammar.

People working on this branch of linguistics are interested above all in how and why language changes. They are also interested in reconstructing an earlier state of affairs in cases where we have no written records of the previous stages of the language.

How language changes

Until relatively recently, language change was considered to be a mysterious, unobservable phenomenon which crept up on one unawares. Like the movement of the planets, it was regarded as undetectable by the unaided human senses. However, advances in sociolinguistics have led to a growing understanding of the mechanisms behind both the spread of change from person to person, and its dissemination through a language.

The American sociolinguist William Labov was one of the first people to examine in detail how a change spreads through a population. He found a new pronunciation creeping in among the permanent inhabitants on the island of Martha's Vineyard, a popular holiday resort off the coast of Massachusetts. Judging by previous accounts of the islanders' speech, the vowel sounds in words such as *I, my* and *out, about* were altering their character, being produced with the mouth considerably less wide open than the standard American pronunciation. Labov did a survey of these vowel sounds, interviewing the islanders, and asking them to read passages containing the crucial words.

He found that the change seemed to be radiating out from a group of fishermen who were regarded as typifying the old true values of the island, in contrast to the despised summer visitors. The fishermen's speech had always been somewhat different from the standard American pronunciation, though in recent years it appeared to have become more extreme. The non-standard vowels were being picked up and imitated in particular by people aged 30–45 who had made a firm decision to stay permanently on the island.

The fishermen's strange vowels, then, were not a totally new invention, they were simply an exaggeration of existing vowels. Other inhabitants who came into contact with these respected old fishermen perhaps subconsciously imitated aspects of their speech in an effort to sound like 'true' islanders. At first, the adopted fisherman-type vowels fluctuated with their existing more standard vowels, then gradually the new ones took over. At this point, the change started to spread to others who came into contact with this second group, and so on.

There is some truth, therefore, in the notion that changes are infectious. Parents sometimes complain that their children 'pick up' dreadful accents at school. But children are not infected against their will. Subconsciously at least, humans imitate those they admire, or desire to be associated with. It is as impossible to stop children acquiring the accents of their friends as it is to stop them wanting to wear the same clothes, or admiring the same pop stars.

Some changes occur 'from above', meaning 'from above the level of consciousness', when people consciously imitate the accent of others. For example, in British English, someone who comes from an area where [h] is omitted at the beginning of words such as *hot, high*, might make a decision to gradually incorporate it, to fit in with the more usual pronunciation. Other changes are 'from below', meaning 'from below the level of consciousness', as with the Martha's Vineyard changes, where those involved might have been unaware of which parts of their speech were changing.

But whether the changes are 'from above' or 'from below', the mechanism of spread from person to person appears to be the same: alternatives creep in, usually copied from those around, then gradually replace the existing pronunciation. Change inevitably involves variant forms while it is in progress, so speech variation is often a sign that a change is taking place.

Spread of change within a language

The spread of a change through the language is a topic which at one time seemed even more mysterious than its spread through a population. One puzzling phenomenon was the so-called 'regularity' of sound change. If one sound changes, the alteration does not only occur in an isolated word. It affects all similar words in which the same sound occurs. So, in English *wyf* became *wife*, just as *lyf* became *life*, and *bryd* became *bride*, all showing a change from [iː] to [aɪ]. In the 19th century, linguists claimed that sound changes were 'laws' which worked with 'blind necessity', sweeping all before them like snow ploughs. But one problem remained. How did odd words get left behind? For example, British English [æ] normally changed into [aː] before [s], as in *pass*, *fast*, *disaster*. So why do we still get *gas*, *mass*, *aster*, *tassel*? It seems very puzzling that these sweeping 'laws' should rush through a language, yet somehow accidentally miss some words.

One answer was to deny that there really were any exceptions and suggest that such words were borrowed from neighbouring dialects. For example, British [æ] in words such as *gas* might be due to American influence. But this feeble attempt to evade the problem was not really satisfactory and, recently, detailed questionnaires and surveys have revealed a better answer.

Linguists have now shown that sound changes do not occur simultaneously in all words at once. They move across the language going from one word to another, like apples on a tree, which ripen round about the same time, but not simultaneously. When charted on a diagram, the progress of the change shows a characteristic S-curve: the time scale goes along the bottom, the number of words affected up the side (Figure 13.1). First, the change touches relatively few words, and affects them variably in that the new pronunciation is likely to exist alongside the old. In the Martha's Vineyard vowels, for example, the word *I* was affected early, but the 'new' pronunciation of *I* did not happen each time, only sometimes. At this point, the change is merely a mild tendency which could be reversed, or even fade out altogether. The words affected early are sometimes the commonest, but phonetic factors are also important: words

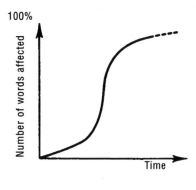

figure 13.1

beginning with vowels tended to be the most affected in Martha's Vineyard. So *I* and *out* were changed early partly because they are common words, partly because of their linguistic shape.

The early stage of a change, with just a few words intermittently affected may last a long time. But, at some point, the change is likely to 'catch on'. It will in all probability then spread fairly fast to a considerable amount of vocabulary, as shown by the steep part of the S in Figure 13.1. Towards the end, a change tends to lose its impetus and peter out, so there may be a few words it never reaches. This scenario, then, of a change creeping from word to word accounts for why changes are for the most part regular, but why some words can get left out. The process is known as **lexical diffusion**. The words affected by a change fluctuate at first, with the new and old pronunciation coexisting. But eventually, the newer pronunciation wins out.

Causes of language change

'There is no more reason for language to change than for jackets to have three buttons one year and two the next', asserted one well-known linguist, arguing that all change is due to accidental, social factors. This viewpoint cannot be correct, for two reasons. First, similar changes recur the world over. There are certain tendencies inherent in language, which possibly get triggered by social factors, but which are there waiting in the wings as it were, for something to set them off, as with an avalanche: a lone skier who disturbed the snow was perhaps the immediate trigger, but deeper underlying causes already existed, before that skier arrived.

Furthermore, language patterning never breaks down. This is the second reason why changes cannot be simply accidental. The patterns within language enable the mind to handle large amounts of linguistic information without strain. If change was random, the organization would collapse. The mind would be overloaded with a junk-heap of disorganized information, and communication would be impossible.

These factors provide two major causes of change: on the one hand, there are underlying tendencies in language, tendencies which can get triggered by social factors. On the other hand, there is a therapeutic tendency, a tendency to make readjustments in order to restore broken patterns. Let us briefly consider these.

Natural tendencies

There are numerous natural tendencies, and some of them are stronger than others. They can be triggered by social factors, or may be held at bay for centuries, perhaps held in check by other opposing tendencies.

A widespread tendency is for the ends of words to disappear. In cases where this has largely occurred already, as in the Polynesian languages, Italian, and French, many English speakers claim the language 'sounds beautiful', 'has flowing sounds'. But when it begins to happen to our own language, and people leave [t] off the end of words such as *hot*, *what*, and replace it with a 'glottal stop' – a closure at the back of the vocal tract with no actual sound emitted – then many people get upset, and talk about 'sloppiness', and 'disgraceful swallowing of sounds'. However, such an incident is certainly not 'sloppiness', since producing a glottal stop requires as much muscular tension as the sound it replaces. Furthermore, the change is creeping in inexorably: even those who criticize it usually fail to notice that they themselves are likely to replace [t] with a glottal stop in *football, hot milk, a bit more*. In some areas, the change has affected [k] as well, and also, to a lesser extent, [p]. At the rate at which it seems to be spreading, [p], [t] and [k] may have disappeared from the end of British English words by the middle of the 21st century.

Not all tendencies are major, noticeable ones. Others can be minor, affecting only one sound in a particular position: the sound [e] tends to become [ɪ] before [ŋ], so *England* is now pronounced as if it were spelled 'Ingland'. A [b] tends to be inserted between [m] and [l], so the word *bramble* is from an earlier *bremel*. And so on.

Some tendencies can have repercussions throughout the language, as with the loss of the ends of words, which means that in French, for example, an alternative means of expressing 'plural' has had to be developed: it is essential to put *les* [le] at the beginning of plural words, as in *les chats* [le ʃa] 'the cats', since by itself the word *chat* [ʃa] 'cat' is pronounced the same in both the singular and plural: this distinction is now marked by the determiner placed in front of words.

Therapeutic changes

Therapeutic changes restore patterns which have been damaged by previous changes. A number of examples of this are provided by the use of **analogy**, the ability to reason from parallel cases, which is a fundamental feature of human language. It is most obvious in the case of child language, when children create past tenses such as *taked*, *drinked*, after hearing forms such as *baked*, *blinked*.

In language change, analogy tends to restore similar forms to items which have become separated by sound changes. For example, changes in the vowel system resulted in the separation of the adjective *old* from its comparative form *elder*. So a new comparative form *older* has been formed by analogy with forms such as *young*, *younger*, where the first part of both words is the same. The form *elder* has now been relegated to a few specialized uses and phrases, such as *elders of the church*, *his elder brother*.

However, it is a mistake to regard analogy purely as a restorer of broken patterns. This is an oversimplification, because analogy is not only found in a therapeutic role: it can itself disrupt sound changes. For example, we would expect [d] in the middle of the word *father* (as in Gothic *fadar*). But *father* was influenced by the word *brother*, and the expected [d] appears as [ð]. In addition, there are a number of different types of analogy. In some ways, it is a 'rag-bag' category used to explain a variety of changes. So it is misleading to make vague general claims about analogy, unless the statement can be narrowed down.

Changes which trigger one another off

Chain shifts – that is, changes which seem to occur in linked sequences – are a particularly interesting therapeutic phenomenon. For example, in Chaucer's time the word *lyf* 'life' was pronounced [liːf] (like today's *leaf*). The vowel [iː] changed to [eɪ] (and later to [aɪ]). But this was not an isolated change. At around this time, all the other long vowels shifted: [eː] became [iː], [ɛː] became [eː], and [aː] became [ɛː]. It looks as if each vowel rushed to fill the empty space left by the one ahead of it (Figure 13.2).

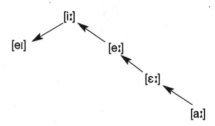

figure 13.2

Yet the situation is not necessarily as straightforward as the example given here – which is itself disputed. Quite often, several sounds move simultaneously, making it difficult to say whether one sound is being dragged into an empty space, or whether it is being pushed out of its rightful place. In Figure 13.3, is [eː] being dragged into the space left by [iː]? Or is it being pushed by [ɛː]?

Controversy surrounds the actual mechanism by which sounds affect one another. The only certain fact is that changes seem to occur in linked sequences, and in so doing preserve the basic patterning of human language.

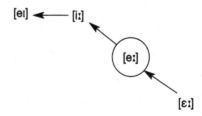

figure 13.3

Recently, linguists have suggested that chain shifts occur not only in the sounds of a language, but in the syntax also, For example, some languages have relative clauses (clauses introduced by *which*, *that*) placed before the nouns attached to them. They say, as it were:

Which is sour wine

where English says 'Wine which is sour'. Such languages also tend to have objects which precede their verbs. A literal translation of English 'Harry dislikes wine which is sour' might be:

Harry [which is sour wine] dislikes.

If, however, a change occurs so that relative clauses move to a position after their nouns, then the verb and object are likely to change places also. Once again, most people would agree that the changes are linked in some way, though the precise mechanism is disputed.

Interacting changes

So far, the changes examined have been fairly straightforward. But some types of change are far more complex. In order to give some idea of the numerous factors normally involved in a language change, let us finally look at some *interacting* changes. In the following example, loss of word endings has combined with changes in word order, to bring about both the disappearance of a construction and a change of meaning.

The forerunner of the English word *like* was *lician*, a verb which meant to 'give pleasure to'. This verb was in common use in English at a time when objects normally preceded the verb, and the subject of the sentence did not necessarily come at the beginning of a sentence. A typical sentence might be:

tham	*cynge*	*licodon*	*peran*
to the	king	gave pleasure	pears

'Pears pleased the king'.

Then, over the course of several centuries, two things happened. First, the noun and verb endings were dropped. *The king* became the standard form for the noun, and the plural ending dropped from the verb. This eventually led to the form:

The king liked pears.

Meanwhile, it gradually became normal to put the subject before the verb, and the object after it. So the sentence 'The king liked pears', which originally meant 'To the king were a pleasure pears', was reinterpreted as 'The king took pleasure in pears'. Therefore, loss of word endings and a word order change have triggered off two further changes: the loss of the construction-type 'to someone, something is a pleasure', and a change of meaning in the word *like* from 'to give pleasure to' to 'to take pleasure in'. This example illustrates the fact that, in most types of language change, a multiplicity of factors are involved.

Reconstruction

Recently, an enormous amount has been found out about language change by examining changes in progress. However, language change is a relatively slow process, so we need in addition to consider how languages have altered over the centuries. Yet our written records are inevitably incomplete. In order to supplement these, historical linguists extend their knowledge by reconstructing stages of language for which there are no written documents.

There are a number of different types of reconstruction. The best known of these is **external reconstruction**, also known as **comparative historical linguistics**. In this, a linguist compares the forms of words in genetically related languages, that is, languages which have developed from some common source, and then draws conclusions about their common ancestor. This type of reconstruction will be discussed further in Chapter 14. An older name for it is 'comparative philology', which sometimes causes confusion, since in the USA, France and Germany, 'philology' normally refers to the study of literary texts.

A second type of reconstruction is known as **internal reconstruction**. In this, linguists look at the state of one language at a single point in time. By comparing elements which are likely to have had a common origin, they are often able to draw conclusions about their earlier form. To take a simple example, consider the words *long* and *longer*. /lɒŋ/ and /lɒŋg/ (with /g/ on the end) are both allomorphs of the morpheme *long*. This suggests that, originally, they were identical, and that the word *long* was once pronounced with [g] at the end (as it still is in some parts of England, such as Liverpool).

A third type of reconstruction is **typological reconstruction**. This is somewhat newer than the other two. Linguists are beginning to be able to divide languages into different types, and to recognize the basic characteristics attached to each type; this branch of linguistics is known as language typology. For example, those languages (such as Hindi) which have verbs after their objects, also tend to have auxiliary verbs after the main verb. On the other hand, languages such as English which have verbs before their objects tend to have auxiliary verbs before the main verb. If, therefore, we were to find the remnants of a language which had its auxiliaries attached after the main verb, we would be able to predict that it might also have its object before the verb, even if we had no direct evidence for this. Typology will be discussed further in Chapter 14.

Let us now see how we might use these three types of reconstruction. Suppose we have three related languages, Twiddle, Twuddle and Twoddle. Let us also assume that we have no past records, merely a record of their present-day speech. First, we would use internal reconstruction (IR) to reconstruct an earlier state of each of these languages – Early Twiddle, Early Twuddle and Early Twoddle. Then we would use external reconstruction (ER) to reconstruct Proto-T, the common ancestor of these three. Then, once again, we would employ internal reconstruction, this time combined with typological reconstruction (TR) to reconstruct an earlier form of Proto-T: Pre-Proto-T (Figure 13.4).

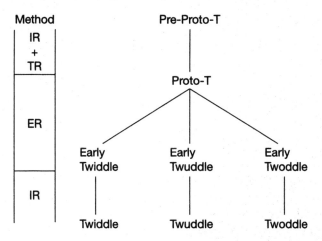

figure 13.4

In this way, we might be able to reconstruct a probable history of these languages stretching over hundreds, and perhaps even thousands of years.

In this chapter, we have considered how and why language changes. We have also briefly looked at how linguists reconstruct past stages for which they have no written evidence. This process will be discussed further in the next chapter.

Questions

1 How do changes spread from person to person?
2 How do changes spread within a language?
3 Suggest two types of causes of language change.
4 What is **analogy**?
5 What is a **chain shift**?
6 Name three types of **reconstruction**, and explain in outline what each involves.

14 comparing languages

This chapter outlines different ways of comparing languages. It discusses the sources of shared features, then sketches the assumptions and methods of comparative historical linguistics, and the reconstruction of the proto-language from which daughter languages developed. It also looks at further ways of extending knowledge of past language stages.

Estimates as to the number of different languages in the world vary considerably, partly because of problems in defining the word 'language' (Chapter 10). The figure most usually quoted is somewhere between 4,000 and 8,000. A few linguists carry out detailed studies of individual languages. Many more, however, are involved in comparing pairs or groups of them. Sometimes they compare them in order to pinpoint dissimilarities (**contrastive linguistics**) and sometimes to identify similarities, which may be due to **universal, genetic, areal** or **typological** factors.

Contrastive linguistics

The comparison of languages in order to find dissimilarities is known as **contrastive linguistics**. It is carried out mainly by **applied linguists,** the name usually given to people who look at the application of linguistic principles to the field of language teaching. It is useful to know in advance where someone learning a language is likely to have difficulties, and these often arise in areas of the 'target' language which are very different from one's own. For example, in Hindi, negation is very simple for the most part. A single negative word is placed before the verb, which is at the end of the sentence:

> *Bill hindustani **nahī** hai.*
> Bill Indian   not   is
> 'Bill is not Indian'.

Because of this, Indian learners of English often have difficulties with the English preference for bringing negatives to the front, and they tend to produce sentences such as:

> *All of these pens don't work.*

where a British English speaker would prefer:

> *None of these pens work.*

Contrastive linguists, therefore, make detailed comparisons of pairs of languages in order to pinpoint dissimilarities. This enables them to predict difficulties likely to be experienced by learners, which will in turn influence the preparation of teaching materials.

Language similarities

In a broad sense, almost all linguists are looking for language similarities, since the search for language universals is one of the major tasks of linguistics. Many linguists, however, study characteristics shared by groups of languages, rather than all of them. **Genetic**, **areal** and **typological** factors are the three main causes behind these shared features. Genetically-based similarities occur when languages are descended from a common ancestor. Areally-based similarities are due to contact between neighbouring languages. And typologically-based similarities occur when languages belong to the same overall 'type'. Let us look at each of these.

Genetic similarities

The search for genetically related languages, and the reconstruction of the hypothetical parent language from which they were descended, was considered to be the most important task of linguistics in the 19th century (Chapter 3). These days, comparative historical linguistics is a branch of historical linguistics (Chapter 13). It enables us to follow through the development of a language from an early stage, and to distinguish inherited features from recent innovations.

It is often not immediately apparent which languages are related. At first glance, Welsh, Spanish and Russian look quite different, yet these are all Indo-European languages. We need to look for **systematic correspondences** between the languages, rather than similar-looking words, which can be misleading. For example, it is mere chance that German *haben* 'have' resembles Latin *habere* 'have'. And Turkish *plaz* 'beach' only sounds like French *plage* 'beach' because it was borrowed from French. On the other hand, *beef* and *cow* are (perhaps surprisingly) related, and so are the words *paradise*, *dough* and *fiction*, which can be traced back to a Proto-Indo-European word meaning 'make, mould, build'.

Two basic assumptions underlie our search for systematic correspondences. First, linguistic symbols are essentially arbitrary. As explained in Chapter 2, there is no connection between the sound of a word and the thing it symbolizes, except in the case of occasional onomatopoeic words. Therefore consistent similarities between languages which cannot be explained by borrowing may be due to common origin. The second assumption is that sound changes are for the most part regular. If one sound changes, then all similar sounds in the same phonetic environment and geographical area change also. On the basis of these two assumptions, we may draw up reliable and systematic correspondences between the various related languages.

The correspondences which we look for can be found either in the sounds, or, more reliably, in the morphology, since it is rare (though not impossible) for one language to borrow another's morphology. Figure 14.1 shows some English and German examples:

German			English
/d/			**/θ/**
dick	fat	←——→	**th**ick
Ding	thing	←——→	**th**ing
Ba**d**	bath	←——→	ba**th**

/ʃv/			**/sw/**
schwimmen	swim	←——→	**sw**im
schwingen	swing	←——→	**sw**ing
Schwan	swan	←——→	**sw**an

figure 14.1

These systematic sound correspondences between words with the same or similar meaning are the first clue that the languages may be related. The evidence is cumulative. The more correspondences, the more likely the languages are to be related. In the German–English example above, the words are fairly similar, but (as already noted) this is not essential. For example, we can recognize the relationship between English and Latin on the basis of correspondences between words such as:

Latin *pater* 'father'	English *father*
pes 'foot'	*foot*

Here Latin *p* consistently corresponds to English *f*.

However, correspondences must never be accepted uncritically. We might be dealing with a series of loanwords which diverged in development after being borrowed. For example, there is a superficial correspondence between:

French *mouton* 'sheep'	English *mutton*
bouton 'button'	*button*
glouton 'glutton'	*glutton*

But these are all words borrowed from French at the time of the Norman invasion. More reliable are morphological correspondences, such as those shown in Figure 14.2.

German

No suffix	/ə/	/ste/
klein	kleiner	kleinste
schnell	schneller	schnellste
reich	reicher	reichste

English

No suffix	/ə/	/est/
small	smaller	smallest
quick	quicker	quickest
rich	richer	richest

figure 14.2

Such correspondences definitely prove that German and English are related. And earlier in this century, Hittite was established as an Indo-European language on the basis of morphological correspondences, in spite of the fact that its vocabulary consists mainly of non-Indo-European words.

Building a family tree

Once we have established that a number of languages are related, then we have to form a hypothesis as to exactly how they are linked. If we find three related or 'cognate' languages, say German, English and French, then we have to decide whether they should form three separate branches from the parent, or whether (as is in fact the case) two of them diverged from one another at a later stage (Figure 14.3, p. 176).

This would affect the reconstruction, because we would then have to reconstruct the ancestor of German and English before moving on to the next stage, that of reconstructing the overall ancestor.

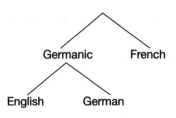

figure 14.3

Reconstructing the parent language

When we have set up a family tree, we can begin to reconstruct. We do this by looking first of all at the 'majority verdict'. That is, we look at the sounds found in daughter languages of a similar age, and, as a first hypothesis, suggest that those on which the majority agree might represent the original sounds. For example, among the Indo-European languages, we find Sanskrit *sapta*, Greek *hepta*, Latin *septem*, all meaning 'seven'. This group of words suggests that the parent language word was perhaps [septa].

Second, our preliminary hypothesis must be checked to see if the developments we have proposed are phonetically probable. We are assuming, for example, that in Greek, [s] changed to [h], that in Sanskrit, [e] changed to [a], and that in Latin [a] changed to [em]. Are such changes possible or likely? In this case, the answer is 'yes' as far as [s] → [h], and [e] → [a] are concerned, but 'no' to [a] → [em], which is highly unlikely. [em → a] would be more probable. Can we propose an original [septem]?

On checking further, we discover that Greek and Sanskrit do not normally lose all trace of [m] at the end of words, so something must be wrong somewhere. A more plausible hypothesis is that the final syllable was originally rather like the sound sometimes heard at the end of English *madam*, in which [m] appears to be behaving in a vowel-like manner. This vowel-like [m] (sometimes written [m̩]) commonly becomes either [a] or [em], so our final reconstruction for the word 'seven' is [septm̩].

As we gradually build up a picture of the proto-language, we need in addition to check whether, in the light of our knowledge of languages in general, we have reconstructed a possible proto-language. If it looks totally unlike any language we have ever seen, then we should be suspicious of our conclusions.

Unreliability of reconstructions

It is, unfortunately, most unlikely that we shall succeed in reconstructing an accurate representation of the parent language. For a start, there are always enormous gaps in the evidence available. In the reconstruction of Proto-Indo-European, linguists rely overmuch on Greek, Latin and Sanskrit because of the extensive written records which have survived. Similar written records of Albanian or Armenian might dramatically change the picture. Second, it is not always possible to deduce the actual pronunciation from written texts, yet our reconstructions are to a large extent based on these texts. Third, no parent language is ever a single, homogeneous whole. Every language has dialectal variations within it, so reconstructions are likely to be hotch-potch forms made up from several dialects. Fourth, daughter languages sometimes undergo independent, parallel developments which can falsify the picture of the parent language. If we possessed only English, Russian and Italian, we might wrongly deduce that Indo-European had a stress accent. But stress developed independently in all three languages after the break-up of the parent language. Fifth, borrowing from neighbours can distort the picture.

In conclusion, we realize that reconstructions merely represent the best guesses we can make about the parent language in the light of current knowledge. No one nowadays has the confidence of the 19th-century scholar who attempted to translate one of Aesop's fables into Proto-Indo-European! Above all, they provide a convenient summary of possible inherited features, so allowing linguists to distinguish long-standing characteristics from recent innovations.

Linguistic areas

When similarities are found between adjacent languages, so-called **borrowing** should be suspected as a possible source. Languages which come into contact with one another often take over some of the linguistic features of their neighbours. Borrowed vocabulary items are particularly common: English has adopted numerous French food words: *courgettes, aubergines, pâté*, for example. Borrowing of constructions is more likely to occur if the languages are structurally similar. But even dissimilar languages can, over time, gradually absorb features from one another. If some particularly striking characteristic has spread over a wide range, linguists sometimes talk about **linguistic areas**.

The reason for studying areal characteristics is twofold: on the one hand, knowledge of how languages can affect one another extends our understanding of language change. On the other hand, it is important to isolate shared features caused by borrowing, so as not to confuse them with genetic and typological similarities.

Areal features can involve any aspect of the language. For example, Chinese, Thai and Vietnamese are all spoken in the Far East, and they are all tone languages, something which has apparently come about through contact. And in India, languages with quite different origins have all developed a particular type of sound, known as a 'retroflex', in which the tongue is curled backwards against the palate.

Several Balkan languages show similarities which appear to be due to proximity. Albanian, Bulgarian and Romanian all have the so-called 'definite article' *the* attached after the noun. For example, Romanian has *munte-le* 'mountain-the', a construction which has clearly been borrowed from its neighbours, since languages to which it is more closely related show the reverse order, as in the historically related French equivalent *le mont* 'the mount'. The same three languages, as well as another neighbour, modern Greek, all say the equivalent of: 'Give me that I eat', when one might have expected them to say 'Give me to eat', judging from other European languages. These particular features seem to have spread during the centuries when Byzantine culture was a unifying force in this part of the world.

Features which are borrowed from another language seep in slowly. This has led to a search for wider-ranging, more ancient borrowings. Linguistic characteristics shared over more extensive parts of the globe might shed light on prehistoric population movements, an approach known as **population typology**.

For example, some languages distinguish between two types of *we*, inclusive *we* which indicates the people in the conversation, and exclusive *we*, which does not:

> *Yesterday we* (inclusive) *arrived.* = I and others present.
> *Yesterday we* (exclusive) *arrived.* = I and others not present.

Hardly any European languages have this distinction, quite a lot of south and east Asian ones have it, and so do most Australian languages. This suggests that it might be a very old feature which has spread slowly westward in the course of centuries.

Language types

Parallel structures in languages may occur because the languages are of a similar type. Just as one can divide human beings into different racial types on the basis of characteristics such as bone structure, skin colour, blood group and so on, so one can divide languages into different groups.

The recent interest in **linguistic typology** has arisen in part out of the failure to find large numbers of language universals. Absolute universals, characteristics shared by all languages, proved to be hard to identify, and those attempting to list them were driven back onto vague statements such as: 'All languages have the means of asking questions'. When people tried to pin these statements down further, such as querying *how* questions were asked, it became clear that certain devices recurred in human languages, though different languages favoured different constructions.

Of course, the observation that different languages use different constructions is by no means new. What is new, is the recent interest in **implicational universals** and implicational tendencies. That is, if a language has a particular construction, it is also likely to have further predictable characteristics. Just as one can say that, if an animal has feathers and a beak, it is also likely to have wings, so one can make statements of the type: 'If a language has a basic pattern of subject, verb, object, it is also likely to have prepositions (rather than postpositions)'.

Morphological criteria for language classification

What criteria should form the basis for language classification? There is considerable controversy about this. The earliest work on the topic, in the 19th century, was based on the way in which morphemes were handled.

The number of morphemes per word varies from language to language – so does the way in which morphemes are combined within a word. In the 19th century, scholars tried to use such criteria for dividing languages into different types. They recognized at least *three* different morphological types.

An **isolating** (or analytical) language is one in which words frequently consist of one morpheme. This is often the case in English:

Will you please let the dog out now.

An **agglutinating** language (from the Latin word for 'glue together') is one in which words can be divided into morphemes without difficulty. Turkish and Swahili are well-known examples. But agglutination is also used to a limited extent in English:

lov-ing-ly   faith-ful-ness

A **fusional** language is one such as Latin which fuses morphemes together in such a way that they are not easily recognizable as separate elements. For example, *-us* on the end of *taurus* 'bull' indicates that it is masculine, singular, and the subject of the sentence, but these three aspects cannot be disentangled. Occasional examples of fusion occur in English:

went = go + past tense

At one time it was thought that languages followed a fixed pattern of development. The first stage was an isolating one, the second agglutinating, the third fusional. Greek and Latin were spoken of in sentimental terms as representing the highest and best of language types. Everything else was regarded as an aberration, or a symptom of decline and decay. The fallacy of such a belief is pointed out vividly by the American anthropologist and linguist Edward Sapir: 'A linguist that insists on talking about the Latin type of morphology as though it were necessarily the high-water mark of linguistic development is like the zoologist that sees in the organic world a huge conspiracy to evolve the race-horse or the Jersey cow.'

The main flaw in the type of classification outlined above is that no language is a 'pure' morphological type. A few languages fit into one category rather than another, but many appear to have mixed morphological processes. So nowadays, most linguists use other criteria for dividing languages into different types.

Word order criteria

English uses word order as a basic syntactic device. In linguistic terminology, it is a **configurational language** (Chapter 7). Perhaps for this reason there has been an enormous amount of interest in word order as a typological characteristic. Among the possible word orders, only a limited number are commonly used, and each of these is likely to possess certain predictable characteristics.

The most usual preliminary classification is in terms of subject, verb, object. In theory, there are six possibilities:

Subject first	*Verb first*	*Object first*
SOV	VSO	OVS
SVO	VOS	OSV

In practice, the ones on the left (subject first) are considerably more common than the ones in the middle (verb first), whereas the ones on the right (object first) are extremely rare. In fact, no sure example of OSV has ever been found, and the few examples of OVS are clustered together in South America.

Examples of languages which fit each of these types, with the literal order in which they would express a sentence *The dog killed the duck* are:

SOV	*The dog the duck killed*	(Turkish).
SVO	*The dog killed the duck*	(English).
VSO	*Killed the dog the duck*	(Welsh).
VOS	*Killed the duck the dog*	(Malagasy (Madagascar)).
OVS	*The duck killed the dog*	(Hixkaryana (S. America)).
OSV	*The duck the dog killed*	(? Apurina (S. America)).

This preliminary classification is useful, but it also presents some problems. The most obvious difficulty is that a number of languages do not fit easily into one of these categories, for various reasons. In some languages, such as the Australian languages Dyirbal and Walbiri, it seems to be impossible to identify a 'basic' word order. These appear to be genuine non-configurational languages: their word order is extremely free and flexible. In other languages, the word order seems to be fixed, but mixed. For example, German has SVO order in main clauses, but SOV in subordinate clauses. It says in effect:

The dog killed the duck (SVO, main clause).
I heard that [the dog the duck killed] (SOV, subordinate clause).

Furthermore, in several languages, it is extremely difficult to identify the 'subject' of the verb. Take the sentences:

The dog killed the duck.
The dog ran away.

In English, *the dog* would be regarded as the subject of both these sentences. But in some languages, such as Inuit, an Eskimo language, *the duck* in the first sentence would be given the same inflectional ending as *the dog* in the second sentence. Situations such as this make it difficult to make reliable decisions about what is a 'subject', and what is an 'object'. The rationale behind the Inuit situation (somewhat simplified) is that there is a standard ending put on most nouns, but this is changed in cases where there are two nouns in a sentence, in which case the more active participant, the 'agent', is given a special ending.

In addition, so-called **pro-drop** languages cause problems. These are languages which can omit pronouns, usually the subject pronoun. In Latin, for example, *canō* 'sing-I' was commoner than *egō canō* 'I sing-I', where the pronoun was added only if extra emphasis was needed. In these languages, the order of verb and object when the pronoun is dropped is not necessarily the same as that of verb and object when S, V, O are all present.

These problems show that word order classifications are not entirely trustworthy. However, statistically, certain probabilities emerge. For example: an SVO language is likely to have auxiliaries preceding the verb, prepositions rather than postpositions, and genitives following the noun, whereas an SOV language is likely to have auxiliary verbs after the verb, postpositions rather than prepositions, and genitives preceding the noun. The English examples on the left would be likely to be represented in an SOV language by the order on the right:

SVO	*Bill eats potatoes.*	SOV	*Bill potatoes eats.*
AUX V	*Marigold can go.*	V AUX	*Marigold go can.*
PREP	*On Saturday.*	POSTP	*Saturday on.*
N GEN	*Queen of Sheba.*	GEN N	*Of Sheba queen.*

Because language is always changing, there are very few languages which are 'pure' types, in the sense of being a perfect example of the statistical probabilities. Most languages have some inconsistencies, and some **doublets** (double possibilities). English, for example, can say *Sheba's queen* as well as *queen of Sheba*.

However, a list of statistical probabilities is only a first stage in the working out of language types. The second, and more important stage, is to find out why these probabilities exist. This is still under discussion, and there may be several interacting explanations. One suggestion is that in languages there is a **principle of cross-category harmony**. That is, different linguistic categories such as nouns, verbs and prepositions, all behave somewhat similarly to one another: the main word or **head** in a phrase is likely to be in a similar position throughout the different types of phrases. For example, if a verb normally occurs at the beginning of the verb phrase, as in English *eats peanuts*, then a preposition is likely to be at the front of its phrase, as in *on Saturday*, and an adjective at the front of its phrase, as in *red in the face*, and a noun at the front of its phrase, as in *father of the family*. Interestingly, the conclusion that languages behave in this way has also been arrived at independently by theoretical linguists trying to describe sentence patterns (X-bar syntax, Chapter 7).

Implicational probabilities can also, with a certain amount of caution, be used to reconstruct probable earlier states, as a supplement to other types of reconstruction in historical linguistics (Chapter 13). If we found traces of an old language which had verbs after objects and postpositions, then we would also be able to say that it was statistically likely to have genitives preceding nouns, for example.

At the moment, there is still an enormous amount more to be done in relation to typological characteristics for classifying languages, and the ensuing implicational relationships. Recently, Chomsky and his followers have started to take an interest in this type of work. Some of these ideas will be discussed in Chapter 18.

Questions

1 What is **contrastive linguistics**?
2 Suggest three reasons why languages might show similarities.
3 How might one recognize genetically related languages?
4 What is the purpose of reconstructing a proto-language?
5 What are **implicational universals**?
6 Which basic word orders are the commonest among the world's languages?

15 attitudes towards change

This chapter discusses language worriers, those who fear that English is declining. It considers why such worries arise, and clarifies the notion of a 'standard language'.

'The language the world is crying out to learn is diseased in its own country', raged a letter-writer to a newspaper. Language worriers pop up repeatedly, fearful for the health of English. These linguachondriacs – language hypochondriacs – often claim that they are defending a language which is collapsing into ruin.

But English is not crumbling away, it is expanding. It is spoken in almost every country in the world, and more speakers are added annually.

So what is the problem? This chapter will consider first, why language worries arise. Second, it will try to clarify the notion of a 'standard language'.

A tradition of worry

Language worriers have always existed. 'Tongues, like governments, have a natural tendency to degeneration', said Samuel Johnson, in the preface to his famous dictionary of the English language, first published in 1755. He at first hoped to halt this presumed decline. But by the time he had completed his work, he realized that 'to enchain syllables' was as pointless as trying 'to lash the wind'.

Eighteenth-century worries were perhaps understandable. At that time, English was in a fairly fluid state, and was thought by many to need stabilizing. This anxiety about English coincided with admiration for Latin, which appeared to be fixed.

But who exactly should say what was, and what was not, good English? A number of church dignitaries thought they knew. In 1762, Robert Lowth, Bishop of London, complained that English 'hath made no advances in Grammatical accuracy' over the last 200 years, criticizing even 'our best Authors' as 'guilty of palpable error in point of Grammar'. He himself tried to remedy this, by writing a grammar of English. Unfortunately, his prescriptions were based partly on Latin, partly on his own personal preferences. For example, he noted that a preposition at the end of sentences was something which 'our language is strongly inclined to', but claimed that it was 'more graceful' to avoid this – even though he himself did not always follow his own advice!

Lowth therefore was one of a long line of well-meaning but ignorant worriers who invented strange personal 'rules' for language, several of which became fossilized in school grammar books.

Progress and decay fallacies

In the 19th century, pride in the British empire led to a mistaken belief that the English language was superior to others. But views differed as to why.

According to one view, English had progressed further than other languages, which remained primitive. 'What shall we say of the Fuegians, whose language is an inarticulate clucking?... Of the wild Veddahs of Ceylon, who have gutturals and grimaces instead of language?' asked a prominent churchman, Dean Farrar, in 1865.

According to another view, God had once created all human languages equal, but some had slithered down from their former excellence. 'Fearful indeed is the impress of degradation which is stamped on the language of the savage', ranted an influential archbishop of Dublin, Richard Chenevix Trench, condemning in particular a language which had supposedly lost its word for 'supreme Divine Being'.

This second view was more pernicious. It promoted three bizarre, wrong ideas: that language and morals are intertwined, that languages can disintegrate, and that constant vigilance is needed to prevent linguistic collapse.

Just as a lost nail is assumed to lead to a lost horseshoe, then a lost horse, then a lost rider, so generations of youngsters have been led to believe that they need to pay attention to linguistic details in order to preserve their language – even though such concern is pointless. Language behaves like a thermostat, and maintains its own patterns (Chapter 13).

Proper behaviour

Further worries surfaced in the 19th century. The inhabitants of England – and also some parts of America – were convinced that a 'proper way' to behave existed. Etiquette books were published with firm precepts on day-to-day life, such as: 'Don't drink from your saucer', 'Don't wear diamonds in the morning', 'Don't conduct correspondence on postal-cards'.

Language was assumed to be part of this 'proper behaviour'. A mish-mash of prohibitions was promoted: 'Don't say gents for gentlemen, nor pants for pantaloons. These are inexcusable vulgarisms', 'Don't use a plural pronoun when a singular is called for. "Every passenger must show their ticket" illustrates a prevalent error', 'Don't say "It is him", say "It is he"'. And so on.

A widespread illusion prevailed, that something called 'correct' English existed, and that this was in some way linked even to morals:

> Speech is a gift of God, ... and the habit of speaking correct English ... next to good morals, is one of the best things in the world,

proclaimed a 19th century manual used by schools.

Exactly what this 'correct English' consisted of was unclear. Those who believed in its existence tended to provide miscellaneous prohibitions against things you should *not*, in their opinion, say, as illustrated above.

Standard English

In the 20th century, a belief in 'proper English' persisted, linked to the notion of a 'standard language'.

The word 'standard' is ambiguous. Sometimes, it means a value which has to be met, as when people talk about 'keeping up standards', or 'reaching the required standard'. At other times, it refers to common practice, as in 'the standard way to make tea is as follows ...'.

Often, these two meanings have been confused, as when a mid-19th-century writer claimed that 'the common standard dialect is that in which all marks of a particular place of birth and residence are lost'.

In practice, standard English was commonly assumed to be the language of Oxford, so-called 'Oxford English', and the big public schools. It therefore came to be thought of as 'educated English'. Henry Wyld, in 1907, noted that 'Standard English ... is spoken by people of corresponding education and cultivation all over the country'.

As Henry Wyld pointed out, standard English refers primarily to written grammatical forms. These vary little from one area to another, even though speakers may differ in pronunciation and vocabulary. Standard English has never been an accent, and people with a Scottish, Welsh or Yorkshire accent are all likely to be using the same 'standard English'.

'Standard English' is often thought of as British English. Yet these days, English has spread around the world. So it is more accurate to speak of standard British English, standard American English, standard Indian English, standard Singapore English, and so on. Each of these has developed its own agreed grammatical forms. In Indian English, for example, the word *enjoy* need not be followed by a noun. An ice-cream seller is likely to say: 'Please enjoy' to someone who buys one. But in England and America, it is more normal to say: 'I hope you enjoy it'.

Non-standard English

Of course, many people speak English that is not standard. A huge amount of attention – and anger – arose when so-called 'Ebonics', a type of black English, was accepted as usable in some California Schools. Amidst the furore, many lost sight of a few straightforward facts.

First, Ebonics is not a new language, it is just an unfashionable variety of English. Second, Ebonics is not in any way defective, just because it is not Standard American English. Linguistically, nothing is wrong with it; its problems are social. Some features of it are more regular than the standard language. For example, the verb *to be* has been neatened up, and runs *I be, you be, he be, we be, they be*. Third, the most notable feature of Ebonics is its vocabulary – though this is recognizably English, as *feel froggy* 'want to fight', *knock boots* 'have sex'. Fourth, confidence in using one variety of English – Ebonics – is likely to lead to a desire to become familiar with other varieties, including perhaps, more fashionable ones.

The overall message is that all varieties of English are equally 'good' in that they are full languages, not defective or damaged ones. But they are not all equally useful or appropriate. Ebonics may be fine for chatting with mates in California. But it might be a disadvantage in London, where people could find it hard to understand, just as speakers with a strong cockney accent might find it difficult to make themselves understood in California.

Ideally, all speakers would be familiar with a variety of accents and dialects so that they could fit in anywhere, just as globe-trotters anywhere need to be equipped with a quiverful of different languages.

Questions

1 Why in the 18th century did people worry about language?
2 How did 19th-century worries about language differ from 18th-century worries?
3 Why is the word **standard** ambiguous?
4 What is **Standard English**?
5 What is **Ebonics**, and what is its relationship to Standard English?

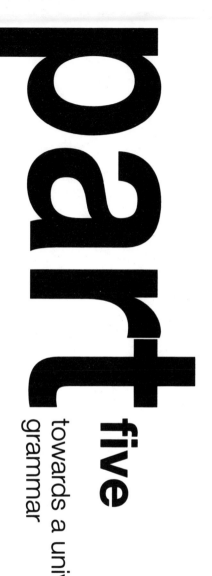

part

five

towards a universal grammar

He that understands grammar in one language, understands it in another as far as the essential properties of Grammar are concerned.

Roger Bacon

16

seeking a
suitable
framework

This chapter considers the
reasons why the linguist Noam
Chomsky set up a
transformational grammar, one
with two levels of structure,
deep and surface, and
explores the basic
characteristics of such a
grammar.

Noam Chomsky has been perhaps the most influential figure in 20th-century linguistics. His contribution has been twofold, as we noted in Chapter 3. On the one hand, he initiated the era of **generative linguistics**, in that he directed attention towards the rules which underlie a person's knowledge of their language. Someone who knows a language is somewhat like a chess-player, who in order to play the game, has had to learn rules which specify which moves are possible, and which not. These rules crystallize the essence of the game. Similarly, the set of rules or 'grammar' underlying a language is, in Chomsky's view, of greater interest than any actual utterances a speaker happens to make.

On the other hand, Chomsky renewed people's interest in **language universals**. This topic was somewhat unfashionable in the early part of the 20th century, when it was commonly assumed that 'Languages differ without limit and in unpredictable ways'. Chomsky argued that linguists should concentrate not so much on finding out components which are common to all languages, which may well be few in number, but on discovering the bounds or **constraints** within which language operates.

Chomsky did not simply make vague statements about the need for generative grammars and universal constraints; he has put forward a number of detailed proposals for a universal framework. Unfortunately for those trying to come to grips with his ideas, he has changed his mind over many facets of his theory since it was first proposed in the 1950s. It started as a **transformational grammar**. In this chapter, we will explain how he arrived at this particular type of grammar in the first place, and sketch out its main characteristics. Then we will consider why he has emended his original ideas (Chapter 17), and finally we will outline some of his more recent proposals (Chapter 18).

Simple models of grammar

Let us now assume that we are in the position that Chomsky was in some years ago – that of a linguist trying to set up a universal grammatical framework. Where should we begin? One fairly obvious way to get going is to write a grammar of a language we know, say, English. If we managed to do this adequately, we could then see to what extent the framework might be used for other languages also. In writing a grammar for English we would adopt the procedure used by all social scientists: we would make a guess or hypothesis, in this case about the rules internalized by someone who knows English. Then we would test the validity of this hypothesis by checking it against some raw data – the sentences of English. If the rules we hypothesized did not lead to good English sentences, they would have to be discarded or amended.

In doing this, we are *not* trying to model the way in which humans prepare a sentence for utterance. A grammar is above all a device which specifies what is, and what is not, a well-formed sentence. It encapsulates rules which define possible sentences, but it does not concern itself with how these possibilities are assembled.

The main task, therefore, is to write a grammar which has the same output as a human being – though there is no guarantee that it will replicate the rules in a person's mind. There will probably be some overlap between a linguist's rules and those actually internalized by human beings, but the mechanisms are unlikely to be identical.

Let us now consider how we might go about forming a hypothesis which would account for the grammar of English. Perhaps the best way is to start with a very simple hypothesis – possibly an over-simple one – and see what flaws it contains. Then, in the light of what we have learnt, we can proceed to a second, more complex hypothesis. And so on.

The simplest possible hypothesis might be to suggest that words are linked together in long chains, with each word attached to the next. For example, the determiners *the* and *a* might be linked to a set of nouns such as *camel*, *elephant*, which in turn might be linked to a set of verbs such as *swallowed*, *ate*, and so on (Figure 16.1).

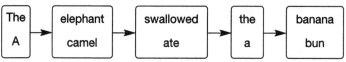

figure 16.1

But we would very quickly have to abandon such a simple model. Neither English, nor any other language, works in this fashion. A word is not necessarily dependent on adjacent words. Often, it depends on another word that is some distance away, as in the sentence:

Either learn to play the trumpet properly or take up yoga.
Petronella fell and hurt herself.

The *or* which is intrinsically connected to *either* appears several words away, not directly after it. Similarly, *herself* which is dependent on *Petronella* is some distance away. Another problem with the 'chain' model above is that it wrongly regards each word as attached to the next by an equal bond. The model fails to show that, in the sentence:

The camel swallowed an apple;

the words *the* and *camel* are more closely related to one another than *swallowed* and *an*. So this simple model must be abandoned.

A somewhat more satisfactory model might be one which treats sentences as if they had a 'layered' structure, as represented in the tree diagrams discussed in Chapter 7. This assumes that languages have several basic sentence patterns, each with a number of different 'slots' which can be expanded in various ways. A noun phrase (NP) followed by a verb phrase (VP) is a basic English sentence type, and this pattern can be expanded in various ways (Figure 16.2).

NP	VP
Ducks	bite
Ducks	bite burglars
The duck	bit the burglar

figure 16.2

Such a grammar (often called a **phrase structure** grammar) contains a series of phrase structure rules, normally in the form of rewrite rules which show the progressive expansions as in Figure 16.3 (see also Chapter 7).

$$S \rightarrow NP \quad VP$$
$$VP \rightarrow V \quad (NP)$$
$$NP \rightarrow D \quad N$$

There seems little doubt that some such expansion mechanism must be built into any grammar. However, according to Chomsky, such a model is incomplete. It contains at least two serious flaws. First, we require an enormous number of rules in

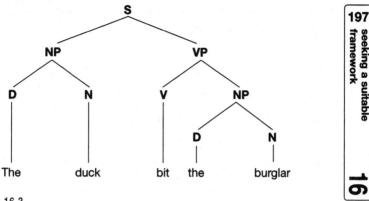

figure 16.3

order to generate all the sentences of English. Second, it groups together sentences which are dissimilar, and separates others which are similar. Take the sentences:

Hezekiah is anxious to help.
Hezekiah is difficult to help.

To someone who knows English, these sentences are radically different. In the first one, Hezekiah is planning to do the helping, and in the other, he is the one liable to be helped. Yet the 'slot' pattern of both is identical (Figure 16.4).

NP	V	ADJ	INF
Hezekiah	is	anxious	to help
Hezekiah	is	difficult	to help

figure 16.4

A similar problem occurs with the sentence:

Hezekiah is ready to eat.

Any English speaker could (with a bit of thought) interpret this sentence in two ways: Hezekiah is hungry, and wants to have his dinner. Or Hezekiah has perhaps fallen into the hands of cannibals, and has been trussed up and seasoned ready for consumption. The slot model, however, cannot easily show the two radically different interpretations.

The reverse problem occurs with pairs of sentences such as:

> *To swallow safety pins is quite stupid.*
> *It is quite stupid to swallow safety pins.*
> *Yesterday it snowed.*
> *It snowed yesterday.*

The sentences in each pair would be regarded as very similar by English speakers, yet this similarity cannot be captured by the model of grammar outlined above, since each sentence requires a different slot pattern.

Chomsky argued that a grammar which provides only one structure for sentences which are felt to be different by native speakers, and different structures for sentences which are felt to be similar, was a bad grammar. A transformational model, he claimed, overcame these problems.

Deep and surface structures

Chomsky's solution to the problem was to suggest that every sentence had two levels of structure, one which was obvious on the **surface**, and another which was **deep** and abstract. Let us see how this works in connection with the sentences discussed on p. 197. Chomsky accounted for the difference between:

> *Hezekiah is anxious to help.*
> *Hezekiah is difficult to help.*

by suggesting that we are dealing with sentences which have a similar **surface structure**, but different **deep structures** (Figure 16.5, where PRES means 'present tense').

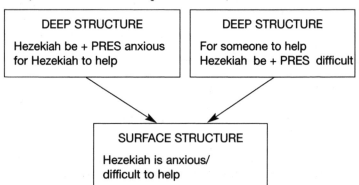

figure 16.5

The deep structures discussed in this chapter are simplified versions of those proposed by Chomsky in his so-called **Standard Theory** of transformational grammar, outlined in his book *Aspects of the Theory of Syntax* (1965).

A similar deep-surface explanation accounts for the ambiguity in:

Hezekiah is ready to eat.

where two different deep structures are realized by a single surface structure. But the situation would be reversed for pairs such as:

Yesterday it snowed.
It snowed yesterday.

Here two different surface structures share a common deep structure (Figure 16.6).

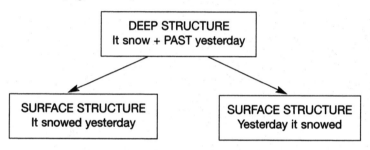

figure 16.6

If every sentence has two levels of structure, then it is clearly necessary to link these two levels in some way. Chomsky suggested that deep structures are related to surface structures by processes called **transformations**. A deep structure is transformed into its related surface structure by the application of one or more transformations. For example, the sentence:

It snowed yesterday.

would require only one transformation – the attachment of the tense to the end of the verb. But the sentence:

Yesterday it snowed.

requires a second one also, one which moves the adverb *yesterday* from the end of the sentence to the beginning.

Transformational grammar

We are now able to give a definition of a **transformational grammar**. It is a grammar which sets up two levels of structure, and relates these levels by means of operations known as **transformations**.

A transformational grammar has (like most other types of grammar) three major components: a syntactic component (dealing with syntax), a phonological component (dealing with sounds) and a semantic component (dealing with meaning). However, it differs from other grammars in that the syntactic component is split into *two* components: the **base**, and the **transformational rules** (Figure 16.7).

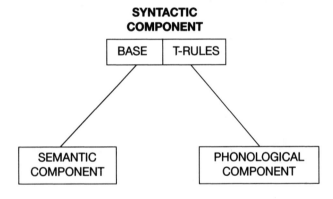

figure 16.7

In the Standard Theory, the base contained phrase structure (PS) rules for the formation of deep structures, and also a lexicon, from which words were slotted into the output of the PS rules (Figure 16.8, p. 201).

The deep structures then passed to the transformational rules in order to be converted into the surface structures. At this point, the surface structure of a sentence was still abstract: it did not yet have a phonetic form. This was coped with by the phonological component, which converted each surface structure into a phonetic representation. Meanwhile, transformations could not change meaning, so the deep structures were fed directly into the semantic component, which gave a semantic interpretation of each (Figure 16.10, p. 202).

BASE (simplified)

PS rules	**Lexicon**
S → NP VP **VP → VP NP** **NP → D N**	elephant **N** king **N** hit **V** [— **NP**] the **D**

DEEP │ STRUCTURE

```
                  S
          ┌───────┴───────┐
         NP              VP
       ┌──┴──┐        ┌───┴───┐
       D     N        V      NP
       │     │        │    ┌──┴──┐
       │     │        │    D     N
       │     │        │    │     │
      the  king      hit  the  elephant
```

figure 16.8

Deep structure

Chomsky did not base his claim that there are two levels of structure purely on the flimsy notion of a native speaker's intuitions.

There were other, more technical reasons. The most important arguments were based on **movement**, cases in which sentence constituents appear to have been moved out of their 'proper' place. Consider the sentence:

Petronella put the parrot in a drawer.

This sentence contains the verb *put* which, as we saw in Chapter 7, has to be followed by both an NP and a PP (Figure 16.9):

NP	**V**	**NP**	**PP**
Petronella	put	the parrot	in a drawer

figure 16.9

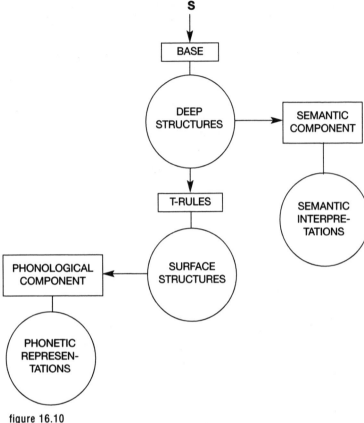

figure 16.10

We cannot say:

* *Petronella put in the drawer.*
* *Petronella put the parrot.*

Now look at the following sentences:

What *did Petronella put* [—] *in the drawer?*
What *did Petronella put the parrot in* [—]?

These sentences appear to have broken the requirements that *put* must be followed by an NP and a PP. Instead, *what* appears at the beginning of the sentence, and there is a gap in the place where one might have expected a word such as *parrot, drawer* to occur.

How are we to deal with these sentences? One possibility is to complicate the lexical entry for *put*, and to say that *put* allows several alternatives:

NP *put* NP PP *(Petronella put the parrot in the drawer.)*
What NP *put* PP *(What did Petronella put in the drawer?)*
What NP *put* NP P *(What did Petronella put the parrot in?)*

Such extra additions to the lexical entry would eventually get extremely complicated, as they would have to take into account cases in which extra sub-sentences had been added between *what* and the original sentence, as in:

What *[did you say] [the police alleged] Petronella had put in the drawer?*

Of course, if the verb *put* was the only lexical item which allowed such manipulations, one might simply put up with this one huge and messy lexical entry. But every verb that is normally followed by an NP allows similar contortions.

Felix grabbed the canary.
What *did Felix grab?*
What *[did Angela claim] Felix grabbed?*

Because of the generality of this occurrence – leaving a 'gap' where an NP was expected, and putting *what* in front of the sentence – it seems more plausible to conclude that it is a general syntactic rule, which says: 'In order to form one common kind of question, substitute *what* in place of an NP, and move it to the front of the sentence.'

If this solution was adopted, one would then hypothesize that the deep structure of the sentences was something like (assuming Q is 'question') (Figure 16.11, p. 204):

Q   *Petronella put **what** in the drawer*
Q   *Petronella put the parrot in **what***

A transformation would then bring *what* to the front, and the sentences would ultimately surface as:

What did Petronella put in the drawer?

What did Petronella put the parrot in?

Such arguments convinced many people that sentences did indeed have two levels of structure: a deep structure and a surface structure linked by transformations.

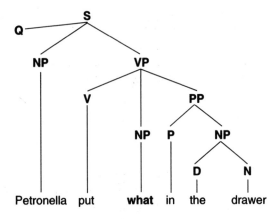

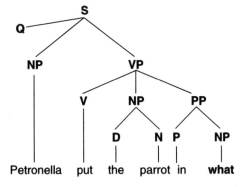

figure 16.11

Transformations

Let us now look more closely at the form which transformations, also known as **T-rules**, took in the (1965) Standard Theory of transformational grammar. Unlike the rewrite rules discussed in Chapter 7, each rule had *two* parts to it. First, an applicability check (usually called the **structural analysis** (SA)) which stated the structure to which the rule could be applied, and second, instructions concerning the change it brought about in this structure (called the **structural change** (SC)) (Figure 16.12):

1	STRUCTURAL ANALYSIS (SA) (applicability check)
2	STRUCTURAL CHANGE (SC) (change brought about)

figure 16.12

Consider, for example, the transformation which moved adverbs to the front of a sentence, **T-adverb preposing**, as in:

Bill shrieked suddenly. → *Suddenly Bill shrieked.*

The structural analysis (applicability check) was needed in order to ensure that the sentence contained an adverb. It said (in more formal terms): 'Check that the sentence contains an adverb'. Once this has been assured, the structural change could be specified. This part of the transformation said (again in more formal terms): 'Move the adverb to the front'.

A formal way of expressing this would be to say:

SA X – ADV
SC X – ADV → ADV – X

Here, X is a 'variable'. This means that its composition can vary. In other words, the structural analysis says: 'The sentence can contain anything you like, as long as it ends in an adverb'. The structural change says: 'X followed by an adverb changes into an adverb followed by X'.

In the Standard Theory of transformational grammar, there were maybe two dozen of these transformations, each applying to a specific structure. In addition to moving things around, as in the examples so far, others deleted items. For example, a command such as *Come!* was assumed to reflect a deeper:

IMP *You will come.*

(where IMP stood for 'imperative'). A T-rule (**T-imperative**) deleted the words *you* and *will*, and the instruction IMP. Other transformations added items. A sentence such as *There is a dodo in the garden* was assumed to reflect a more basic:

A dodo be + PRES in the garden.

A **T-there-insertion** transformation added *there*.

In the 1960s, confident researchers thought that sooner or later, we would compile a definitive list of all the transformations of English, and a complete specification of how they worked. Unfortunately, however, this ambitious programme was never fulfilled, for reasons which will be discussed in the next chapter.

Summary

This chapter has considered the reasons why Chomsky set up a transformational grammar in the first place, and also discussed further reasons in support of the claim that there are two levels of structure, deep structure and surface structure. It also looked in outline at the characteristics of transformations in the Standard Model of transformational grammar.

In the next chapter, we shall consider why the Standard Theory had to be revised.

Questions

1 Define a **transformational grammar**.
2 What arguments could be put forward to support the claim that languages have **deep structures** as well as **surface structures**?
3 How many parts do **T-rules** consist of, and what is the purpose of each of these?

trouble with transformations

This chapter discusses the problems which arose with transformations. Attempts to limit their power proved impossible to specify. As a result, Chomsky started to look at general constraints, ways of preventing grammars from being able to do anything and everything.

Transformational grammar (TG) transformed linguistics, so it seemed. All linguists now had to do was to agree on the form which deep structures took, which were assumed to vary relatively little from language to language. They also had to produce a final and definitive list of possible transformations. At least, that was the general hope in the 1960s. However, little by little, problems crept in. Let us consider why.

Waving a magic wand

The most obvious trouble with transformations in the Standard Theory (1965) was that they appeared to be a kind of magic wand, something which could change a deep structure into any kind of surface structure by any means whatsoever. But this would clearly be absurd. We would not want a device which altered a deep structure something like:

Bill kept the dodo in the bath.

into, say,

My goldfish eats bumble-bees.

There must obviously be some limits on the operations which transformations can perform. The search for the limits or **constraints** which must be placed on them ultimately led to a fundamental reorganization of TG. In this chapter we will look at how this has happened, showing how cracks appeared in what at first looked like a magnificent theory.

Preserving the meaning

In the Standard Model of TG, the strongest constraint placed on transformations (T-rules) was that they should not be allowed to change meaning. One could therefore alter:

Bill kept a dodo in the bath.

into

A dodo was kept in the bath by Bill.
What Bill kept in the bath was a dodo.
In the bath Bill kept a dodo.

These alterations were simply stylistic nuances. They did not alter the basic proposition, that Bill kept a dodo in the bath. There was no change in the lexical items, or in who did what to whom: *Bill* remained the 'agent', the person doing the keeping, and the *dodo* was still the 'patient', the recipient of Bill's action.

This, however, was where the problem started. Certain basic transformations changed the meaning of the deep structure, as in the following examples.

First of all, consider **T-passive**, the T-rule which related active and passive sentences. Look at the active and passive pair:

active: *Many cowboys do not ride horses.*
passive: *Horses are not ridden by many cowboys.*

This pair, according to the Standard Theory, shared a common deep structure, so they should mean the same thing. Yet the reaction of many English speakers is that the two sentences have different interpretations. The active sentence implies that, although many cowboys do not ride horses, many still do. The passive sentence, however, suggests that hardly any cowboys ride horses.

This problem is not necessarily insoluble. One way out of the dilemma was to claim that both sentences have *two* meanings:

1 *Many cowboys do not ride horses, although many still do.*
2 *Many cowboys do not ride horses, and hardly any still do.*

The position of the word *many* in the sentence biases the interpretation of the active towards 1, and of the passive towards 2 – though in theory either meaning is possible for each sentence.

But when different transformations are involved, the problems cannot be explained away so easily, as with another pair of sentences which share a common deep structure, involving a transformation known as **T-conjunction reduction**. This optionally eliminated repeated elements in sentences joined by *and*:

Few women are rich and few women are famous.
Few women are rich and famous.

In the second sentence, **T-conjunction reduction** has optionally been applied, and produced a sentence with a different meaning. If transformations do not change meaning, this should not happen.

These examples show that the problem is a serious one. How can this dilemma be solved? One way out was to suggest that there is something odd about the sentences above: they involve **quantifiers** – words such as *many*, *few*, which express a quantity. In this case, we could assume that transformations change meaning in certain circumstances, one of them being the presence of a quantifier.

This was the solution adopted by a number of linguists, who called their revised grammar the **Extended Standard Theory** (**EST**), since it represented an extension of the Standard Theory, in which (as noted above) transformations could not change meaning.

A second possible response, made by another group of linguists, was to maintain that transformations preserved meaning, but assume that the deep structure had been wrongly formulated in the first place (Figure 17.1). This viewpoint became known as **Generative Semantics** (**GS**), for reasons which will become apparent below.

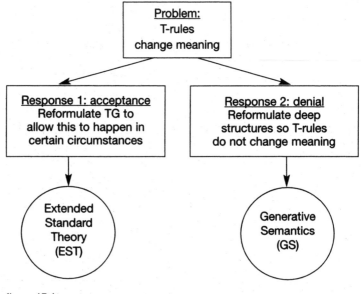

figure 17.1

Generative semantics

The group of people who refused to accept the Extended Standard Theory (EST) claimed that the problem of T-rules which seemed to change meaning lay not so much with the T-rules themselves, as with Chomsky's conception of deep structure, which, they asserted, was insufficiently subtle. It should be elaborated so that each member of the pairs of sentences discussed above has a different deep structure. For example, they denied that the pairs:

Few women are rich and few are famous.
Few women are rich and famous.

shared a common deep structure. If these sentences had different meanings, then they *must* have different **underlying structures** (as the generative semanticists preferred to call deep structures). It was crucial for the underlying structures to deal in more detail with the 'scope' of quantifiers, the parts of the structure affected by words such as *few*, *many*. The main problem was to decide what these complicated and subtle underlying structures were like.

Generative semanticists, however, did not only argue that if two sentences have different meanings, they must have different underlying structures. They also argued (contrary to the Standard Theory) that if two sentences have the same meaning, they must also have the same underlying structure. Consider the sentences:

Henry stopped Drusilla.
Henry caused Drusilla to stop.

According to the Standard Theory, the deep structures would look fairly different. The first consists of only one underlying sentence, the second of two (Figure 17.2):

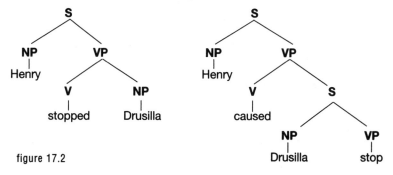

figure 17.2

According to the generative semanticists, the difference between the two sentences was purely superficial. The similarity between them could be represented if the words were decomposed into their component parts. That is, generative semanticists abandoned the assumption (made in the Standard Theory) that lexical items in the deep structure were unanalyzable units.

Instead, they analyzed a word such as *stop* in *Henry stopped Drusilla* into CAUSE STOP, and a word such as *kill* into CAUSE DIE (or, more accurately, into CAUSE BECOME NOT ALIVE), and a word such as *remind* into STRIKE AS SIMILAR TO. Then a special type of transformation packaged up the various components into a single word.

Overall then, generative semanticists gradually elaborated their underlying structures, so much so that eventually they became indistinguishable from semantic structures. This had crucial consequences for the grammar. If underlying structures were the same as semantic structures, then clearly there was no need for them to be separate components within a grammar. The base would initiate or generate a set of underlying structures which *was* the semantic structure. For this reason, those who upheld such a theory were known as **generative semanticists**.

The general idea behind generative semantics was superficially appealing. It seemed common-sensical to many people that meanings should come first, and syntactic means of expressing them follow. Remember, however, these linguists were not talking about the processes involved in producing speech. In writing a grammar, their primary aim was to specify what was, or was not, a well-formed sentence of English. And this became increasingly difficult within the generative semantics framework.

The main problem was that of specifying the underlying structures, which became more and more unwieldy. Nobody could agree on what they should be like, and they seemed to reflect above all the intuitions of the linguists writing them, rather than any objective reality. Furthermore, they required extraordinarily complicated rules for showing how the varying sections of the underlying structure should be combined. In the end, most supporters of this approach gradually gave up on the impossible task of specifying the details.

Trace theory

Eventually, the majority of TG adherents turned away from generative semantics, and admitted that at least some surface structures were important for the interpretation of meaning. Building this possibility into the grammar resulted, as mentioned above, in the **Extended Standard Theory (EST)**. As research continued, many linguists came eventually to the conclusion that the surface structure alone was responsible for meaning, and the resulting amended grammar became known as the **Revised Extended Standard Theory (REST)**.

However, the assumption that surface structures alone are responsible for meaning had several repercussions on the rest of the grammar. Above all, it became important to know where items had been moved from in the deep structure. This was necessary in order for the grammar to be able to deal with the meaning of sentences in which an NP had been shifted away from its original position, as when *what* had been switched to the front. When an NP was moved, therefore, it was assumed to leave behind a faint **trace** of its previous location, marked conventionally by the letter **t** for 'trace'. So, a deep structure something like:

*Q   Drusilla find **what** in the cave.* (Figure 17.3)

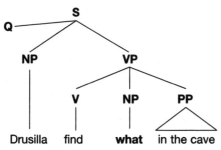

figure 17.3

would have a surface structure something like:

*What (did) Drusilla find **t** in the cave?* (Figure 17.4)

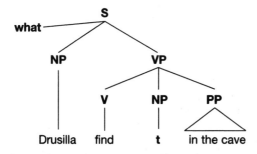

figure 17.4

(Both the deep structure and the surface structure have been considerably simplified here, as elsewhere in this book: only the features relevant to the point under discussion are included.)

Limiting the power of transformations

Remember, the main constraint on T-rules in the Standard Theory was that they could not change meaning. All the meaning resided in the deep structure, and this had to be retained in the surface structure. But in this later version of TG (REST), the surface structures alone provided the semantic interpretation. Therefore linguists were left with the problem they started out with. How could they limit the power of transformations, and prevent them creating a hopeless morass of randomly moved items? It therefore became important to provide firm guidelines as to what could move where. One proposal was that transformations could only move items around within the structure already set up by the phrase structure rules: they could not create a totally new set of structures. In linguistic terminology, they had to be 'structure-preserving' – and a subsidiary effect of this was to alter some of the phrase structure rules.

Another proposal was to limit the distance which items could travel, so that except in exceptional circumstances, they were unable to hop too far away from their own clause. For example, take the sentence:

The discovery that the picture of the aardvark had been stolen was quite upsetting.

The phrase *of the aardvark* was forbidden to hop outside the whole structure:

*The discovery that the picture had been stolen was quite upsetting of the aardvark.

A major preoccupation of linguists working on REST, then, was working out ways of constraining the power of transformations, in particular, ways of preventing items from moving uncontrollably in all directions. But this lack of constraints was not the only problem.

Sharing out the work

A major advantage of Standard TG was that it appeared to simplify the superficial confusion of language. Instead of listing numerous sentence types, it specified a few basic patterns, and the remainder were treated as variants of these basic few.

However, in order to cope with these variants, there were literally dozens of different transformations. This large number raised its own set of problems. Above all, listing umpteen transformations which specified how to produce variants of the basic patterns was not necessarily any more economical than listing different patterns in the first place.

A further problem was that different T-rules sometimes had the same effect, yet this was not recognized in the grammar. Take the sentences:

Marigold was impossible to please.
Bill seems to be ill.

The surface structure subjects (*Marigold, Bill*) had been brought to the front by a transformation, the deep structure of each sentence being something like:

*It was impossible to please **Marigold**.*
*It seems that **Bill** is ill.*

Yet the transformations were quite separate, because they applied to different structures: in the first, *Marigold* is the 'object' of the verb *please*, in the second, *Bill* is the 'subject' of *is*. There was no indication in the grammar that the transformations might be linked, even though they performed similar operations.

These two problems: the large number of different transformations, and the fact that some of them appeared to have the same effect led people to re-examine the transformations one by one. They came to two general conclusions: first, some transformations were not 'proper' transformations, and the operations they performed could be dealt with better in some other component of the grammar. Second, some of the remaining transformations could be combined. Let us briefly look at the offloading and combining which took place.

Offloading

The lexicon and the semantic component were the two components which were seemingly underworked in the existing grammar, and onto which some of the existing transformations were offloaded. Consider the following sentences:

> *Arabella gave the champagne to Charlie.*
> *Arabella gave Charlie the champagne.*

In a Standard TG, the deep structure was somewhat like the first sentence. In order to arrive at the second, a transformation switched the words *champagne* and *Charlie*, and deleted the intervening *to*. But specifying this transformation turned out to be rather difficult. It certainly didn't seem to be a general rule applying to the structure V NP PP. After all, you could say:

> *Arabella took the picnic to the wood.*
> *Jim donated the book to the library.*
> *The TV station transmitted the programme to Japan.*

but not:

> **Arabella took the wood the picnic.*
> **Jim donated the library the book.*
> **The TV station transmitted Japan the programme.*

In brief, this proposed transformation applies just to a few lexical items, such as *give, tell, offer*. It seems somewhat strange to have a T-rule, which is meant to be a general syntactic rule, narrowed down in this way. The lexicon might be a more obvious place for information about the structures following a few verbs. A number of 'transformations', therefore, were reassigned to the lexicon.

Other transformations were reassigned to the semantic component. For example, a Standard TG assumed that the sentence:

> *Antonio claimed that he was ill.*

had a deep structure something like:

> *Antonio claimed that Antonio was ill.*

Then a transformation changed the second *Antonio* to *he*. But this is a fairly unnecessary complication. A simpler alternative would be to have *he* in the deep structure to begin with, but to keep an index of NPs as they occurred, noting which ones are 'coindexed', that is, refer to the same person or thing. This would allow the semantic component to make the correct interpretation at a later stage, without any extra transformational complexities.

In general, then, the transformational component was gradually whittled down as tasks previously dealt with by transformations were offloaded onto other components in the grammar, especially the lexicon and the semantic component.

Combining

As the various transformations were peeled off, only two major processes remained: transformations which moved *wh-* (*what*, *which*, etc.) around, and transformations which moved NPs around as in:

> *What did Arabella buy?*
> *Arabella was difficult to please.*

which had deep structures something like:

> *Q   Arabella bought **what**.*
> *It was difficult to please **Arabella**.*

Yet even these two types of transformation had certain features in common, in that they both moved items to the front. Perhaps, therefore, it was suggested, there was just one basic transformation, which says: 'Items can be moved', instead of lots of different transformations, each of which had to be specified separately. This general transformation then would have to be combined with some clearly stated principles about what could be moved where. This marked a distinct change of emphasis in the grammar. It now relied on general **principles** almost more than on individual rules.

Summary

Let us now summarize: people started with the general problem that transformations appeared to be able to do anything. Moreover, there seemed to be dozens of these powerful devices.

At first, it was hoped to constrain the power of transformations by not allowing them to change meaning, but this proved to be impossible. They clearly did change meaning in a number of cases. This therefore triggered a search for new constraints, principles which would prevent them from altering sentences around in random ways.

As people sought to specify constraints, they realized that the transformations themselves were something of a ragbag, and that a number of them should be removed from the transformational component, since the task they did would be better achieved within another component of the grammar. In this way both the lexicon and the semantic component became more important.

Transformations, meanwhile, dropped off one after the other. In the long run, only one major T-rule remained, which said in effect 'anything can be moved', but which was combined with strong constraints on what could be moved where.

These alterations paved the way for a fundamentally new version of transformational grammar, which will be the topic of the next chapter.

Questions

1 What was wrong with transformations in the Standard Theory of TG, and how did linguists hope at first to solve the problem?

2 What were the basic beliefs of **generative semanticists**, and why did they prove unsatisfactory?

3 What are **constraints**, and why are they necessary in a grammar?

4 Outline two ways in which the number of transformations was reduced.

5 What are **traces**?

6 How many major transformations eventually remained in TG?

back to basics

This chapter looks at the type of grammar Chomsky has finally decided is needed: a principles and parameters model. It outlines the basic principles of such a grammar, which he argues are innate, and then suggests that each language picks from a set of options. Each option implicates certain further choices, which makes languages superficially look very different from one another.

'There are three things in life you must never run after: a bus, a woman and a theory of transformational grammar. There will be another one along in a moment', commented one well-known linguist. Chomsky's 1980s grammar – his so-called **Government and Binding (GB)** approach – was radically different from the Standard Theory, and his 1990s proposals – his **Minimalist Program** – are further away still. In his latest version, he has even abandoned transformations!

This chapter presents a bird's-eye view of his recent ideas. It explains what the grammar is trying to do in general, and glosses over the intricate technical details. More information on these are presented in the works suggested for further reading at the end of the book.

Universal Grammar (UG)

Chomsky has become particularly concerned with the **learnability problem**. How do children manage to learn language so efficiently? They must, he assumes, be born equipped with **Universal Grammar** (UG), a basic outline knowledge of key language properties.

But if UG is inbuilt in the brain, why are languages so different from one another? UG, he argues, is only partially wired up. Children are born with an inbuilt knowledge of basic linguistic **principles**, but these need supplementing. The inherited framework must be backed up with 'parameters that have to be fixed by experience'. A **parameter** is an essential property with inbuilt variation. For example, temperature is a parameter of the atmosphere: temperature must always exist, but is set each day at different levels.

Perhaps youngsters are faced with an array of linguistic switches, he suggests, which have to be switched one way or another. They would instinctively know the basic options, but would need to find out which had been selected by the language they were learning.

Once they had discovered this, multiple repercussions would follow – just as if, say, animals had to opt for air or water as their basic environment, which would in turn bring about a number of inevitable consequences. A simple decision to choose one option rather than another at a particular point would have repercussions throughout the grammar. Relatively few decisions may need to be made, but they would have far-reaching effects.

Chomsky labelled this framework a **Principles and Parameters (P and P) model**, and it features in all his recent work (see Figure 18.1).

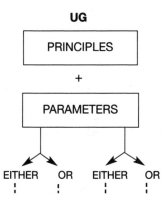

figure 18.1

The possible option points are still speculative, though some suggestions have been made. For example, within phrases, one possible choice might be between having the **head** (main word) at the beginning of a phrase (as in English PP *up the tree*) or at the end (as in Turkish, which says, as it were, *the tree up*). This would have far-reaching effects on the form of sentences. For example, an English sentence such as:

The man who fell downstairs broke his leg.

would, in a language such as Turkish, turn out to have a literal translation, something like:

The downstairs-fell man his leg broke.

Pro-drop might be another crucial option. There might be an important division between languages which allow their speakers to drop the pronouns at the beginning of a sentence, and those which do not. For example, Italian is a pro-drop language. It is possible to say either:

Sono Inglese.   or   *Io sono Inglese.*
am English   I am English

In English, only the second option, the one with the pronoun, is possible. The path taken would have repercussions throughout the grammar, some of them unexpected ones. For example, consider the English sentence:

Angela thought that Hezekiah was stupid.

This has a corresponding question:

Who did Angela think was stupid?

For some strange reason, the word *that* has to be omitted in the question. You cannot say:

*Who did Angela think that was stupid?

This odd fact seems to be characteristic of non-pro-drop languages. Pro-drop languages such as Italian seem able to leave the *that* in.

In the long run, linguists hope to specify all of the crucial option points, and their repercussions. These then would have to be built into the overall framework. If this is ever achieved, then linguists will have gone a long way towards achieving their ultimate goal of specifying UG.

From deep structure to D-structure

Superficially, the most obvious difference between the 1980s TG and the 1960s Standard one was the renaming of some of the essential ingredients, so as not to confuse them with the old ones. Deep structure in its altered form was relabelled **D-structure**, and the revised surface structure was relabelled **S-structure**. The old semantic representation was superseded by **LF** 'logical form', and the phonetic representation was labelled **PF** 'phonetic form' (Figure 18.2).

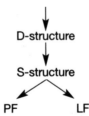

figure 18.2

These levels were linked by processes which had certain superficial resemblances to the older-style TG: PS rules specified the D-structure. D-structure and S-structure were linked by transformational operations, though (as discussed in the previous chapter) the transformational component was a mere shadow of its former self. PF rules converted the S-structure into PF, and LF rules converted the S-structure into LF (Figure 18.3).

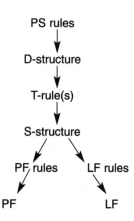

figure 18.3

However, not one of these levels was truly similar to the comparable level in an old style TG, nor were the rules which operate on them the same. For example, the LF rules and LF contain a considerable amount of material which belonged strictly to the syntax in a Standard TG.

Government and binding

The new-look 1980s grammar was presented by Chomsky in a series of lectures published under the title: *Lectures on government and binding* (1981). The name has stuck. It is usually referred to as **government-binding theory**, or GB. This somewhat strange label was because GB paid particular attention to two aspects of grammar which were virtually ignored in the Standard Theory, **government** on the one hand, and **binding** on the other. Government involved the notion of a constituent having power over others, and binding dealt with the linking or binding of items to one another. Let us briefly outline what each involved.

The general notion of government has been around in linguistics for a long time, in that it has long been recognized that some words have influence over, or govern other words. In Latin grammars, for example, grammarians spoke of prepositions governing nouns, since a preposition such as *contra* 'against', as in 'fight against the Gauls', caused the following word, *Gauls*, to have a particular ending. In the more recent (somewhat altered) usage, the word **government** was usually used in connection with heads of phrases which influenced others in their immediate locality, in the sense of requiring them to exist. For example, in English, a verb such as *hit* governs a following NP, as in *hit the donkey*, and a preposition such as *up* also governs an NP, as in *up the tree*. The nodes involved are normally sisters, daughters of the same mother (Chapter 7).

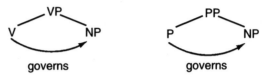

figure 18.4

However, quite often there is an important relationship between words which are on different branches and on different levels, as in the sentence:

Drusilla had a dream about herself (Figure 18.5).

Drusilla and *herself* are on different branches, and different levels, yet clearly they have an intimate relationship, which needs to be carefully specified, since one could not randomly alter the sentence around. It is impossible to say, for example:

*Herself had a dream about Drusilla.
*Drusilla had a dream about Peter kissing herself.

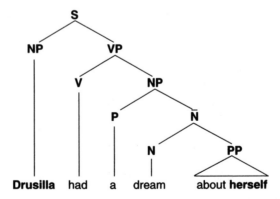

figure 18.5

Furthermore, it is important to understand the relationship in order to interpret sentences properly. Consider the sentences:

Henry read the report about Toby stabbing himself.
Henry read the report about Toby stabbing him.

It is essential to realize that Toby was stabbed in the first sentence, but Henry (or someone else) in the second.

A major part of Chomsky's GB theory was to try and specify exactly which parts of trees influence one another, and which can be linked in their interpretation. He and his followers tried to draw up a wider notion of government, known as **command**. A principle known as **c-command** (from 'constituent command') specified which constituents have power over others in a total tree structure. There was some dispute about exactly how to phrase c-command, but in general (and somewhat simplified), it said that when a node branched, items on the first branch had some influence over those on the second branch, irrespective of how high or low on the tree they came. So, in Figure 18.5 (p. 224), the first NP *Drusilla* c-commands the VP, and every node under it. The main verb *had* c-commands the NP following, and every node under it, and so on.

The notion of c-command enabled one to specify relationships and restrictions between different parts of the sentence. For example, one could say that the word *herself* in the sentence about Drusilla must be c-commanded by the person referred to. This would preclude impossible sentences such as:

*Herself had a dream about Drusilla.

Furthermore, the notion could be used with other constructions, such as:

The politicians argued with one another.

One could specify that a phrase such as *one another* must be c-commanded by the phrase it refers back to, so precluding:

*Each other argued with the politicians.

More generally, one could say that words which refer back to others, traditionally known as **anaphors**, have to be c-commanded by the words they refer back to, their **antecedents**. Therefore, a general structural relationship, that of c-command, could enable one to specify quite simply a large number of apparently separate restrictions, which would have had to be stated one by one in an old style transformational grammar.

Binding is strongly interlinked with the notion of c-command. Briefly, a **binding principle** stated that when two NPs are **co-indexed** – refer to the same thing or person, as with *Marigold* and *herself* in *Marigold cut herself* – then the antecedent (*Marigold*) must c-command the anaphor (*herself*). If so, it has been **properly bound**: in other words, there was a proper link between the two NPs. In contrast, a sequence such as:

*Herself cut Marigold.

would be impossible, because *herself* was not properly bound. Binding related above all to the interpretation of sentences, since it showed which items were to be interpreted as linked together.

All this may seem somewhat like common sense, given these simple examples, and it looks at first sight as if one could just rephrase all this by saying antecedents come before anaphors. But the necessity of specifying a structural relationship between NPs becomes apparent as sentences get more complex, as in:

*Who did Marigold claim cut **herself**?*

The surface structure of this sentence would be something like:

*Who did Marigold claim **t** cut **herself**.*

We need fairly detailed mechanisms to specify the linking of *herself* and *t*, and *t* and *who*, so allowing one to interpret *who* and *herself* together, rather than *Marigold* and *herself* (**t** for 'trace' was explained on p. 213).

To summarize so far, the government and binding approach was particularly concerned about relationships between constituents. It specified which constituents had power over others, the overall purpose being to express simply and clearly which nodes on a tree were interlinked. Only certain links were possible, and discovering and describing these clarified the principles underlying sentence interpretation.

Broadening the range

The Government and Binding (GB) model showed a shift of perspective. In the early days of transformational grammar, a grammar was essentially a device which specified what was, and what was not, a well-formed sentence. In this GB version, Chomsky moved the emphasis to the general principles and relationships which exist within language.

The GB model was the first within the Principles and Parameters (P and P) framework (p. 221). It contained a number of different components, or **modules**, each of which played a role in the whole. For example, **theta-theory** or **θ-theory** – short for 'thematic relations theory' – dealt with who did what to whom by specifying the roles played by NPs, such as **agent** or **theme** (Chapter 7). **The Empty Category Principle (ECP)** specified how to deal with apparent gaps in the structures, as in:

Aloysius wants – to go.

The person who Aloysius wants to go is not overtly specified, yet native speakers know that it is Aloysius.

But considerable arguments arose as to which modules did what, and conflicting proposals were made by different researchers. Chomsky himself proposed some amendments to the theory in his book *Barriers* (1986). But in his recent work, *The minimalist program* (1995), he has largely given up on deciding the tasks allotted to each module.

The bare bones

Chomsky has tried to pare down his linguistic theory to the bare bones of language, which is why he refers to his latest work as a **Minimalist Program**. He is trying to find basic laws of nature, such as a linguistic equivalent of the law of gravity (Chapter 3).

The main feature retained is the switch-setting of the Principles and Parameters (P and P) approach. Two levels of structure have been abolished: D-structure (the descendant of deep structure) and S-structure (the descendant of surface structure) no longer appear.

In this bare bones model, the lexicon feeds into a 'computational system'. This checks that the word combinations are in accord with basic linguistic principles. The lexicon also feeds into a 'spell-out' which specifies the pronunciation. The end-point is meaning on the one hand, and pronunciation on the other (Figure 18.6, p. 228).

The linguistic principles which guide the system are still only sketchy, but they are essentially principles of 'economy' or simplicity. The most straightforward is **Shortest Move**.

Consider the sentence:

Angela has asked Henry to find her hat.

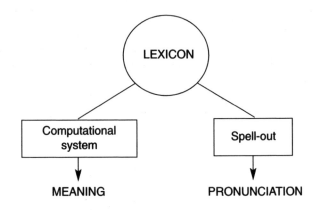

figure 18.6

Suppose you wanted to query *who* Angela had asked and *what* she wanted found:

> *Angela has asked who to find what?*

Normally, any word beginning with *wh* is brought to the front of a sentence. But in this case, only the *wh*-word which moves the shortest distance can come forward: it is possible to say:

> **Who** has Angela asked to find what?

But is impossible to say:

> ****What** has Angela asked who to find?*

This is the type of broad-ranging linguistic principle which Chomsky is hoping to identify, though, as he himself admits, much remains to be done. 'Current formulation of such ideas still leaves substantial gaps', he comments.

Future prospects

Chomsky's model of language is not the only model being worked on, as was pointed out in Chapter 3. However, it still has more adherents than any other model, which is why it has been given prominence in this book.

Questions

1 What is meant by **Principles and Parameters** (P and P)?
2 What do the terms **D-structure**, **S-structure**, **LF** and **PF** mean?
3 What do the terms **government** and **c-command** mean?
4 What is the **Minimalist Program**?

epilogue

But what about ...??? Inevitably, many things have to be left out of a short book. But in some cases, the omissions are more apparent than real. Sometimes so-called 'branches' of linguistics are really assemblages of selected information. Take **applied linguistics** (linguistics and language teaching): in its early years, this involved mainly contrastive linguistics, the comparison of two languages in order to pinpoint their differences (Chapter 14). But in recent years this narrow study has been supplemented by material from pragmatics (Chapter 9), sociolinguistics (Chapter 10) and psycholinguistics (Chapter 11). Similarly, **anthropological linguistics** combines aspects of semantics (Chapter 8), pragmatics, sociolinguistics and psycholinguistics. So even people who feel their interests have been neglected are likely to have found relevant information.

Nevertheless, there is a lot more to linguistics than the contents of this book. Hopefully readers will be able to move on by following up the suggestions in Further Reading (p. 231).

Happy reading!

further reading

These are mostly books which were published relatively recently, usually in the last 10 years. Of course, numerous excellent books were published earlier. But it is possibly more useful to start with the current day, and work backwards. Anyone who starts at the beginning might never get to the end! These suggestions begin with general books, then move on to more specialized topics, mostly in the order in which they are dealt with in this book.

Other introductions

Aitchison, J. *The language web: The power and problem of words.* (Cambridge: Cambridge University Press, 1997).
A readable introduction to language, based on radio talks (the BBC Reith lectures 1996).

Aitchison, J. *The seeds of speech: Language origin and evolution.* (Cambridge: Cambridge University Press, 1996).
An introduction from a new angle: it follows the birth and expansion of language from its earliest origins.

Akmajian, A., Demers, R.A., Farmer, A.K. and Harnish, R.M. *Linguistics: an introduction to language and communication*, 5th edition. (Cambridge, MA: MIT Press, 2001).
A wide-ranging but fairly easy to read introduction.

Bauer, L. and Trudgill, P. (eds.) *Language myths.* (London: Penguin, 1998).
A readable small book which debunks common false beliefs about language.

Cook, V. *Inside language.* (London: Arnold, 1997).
A short, matter-of-fact introduction.

Fromkin, V., Rodman, R. and Hyams, N. *An introduction to language*, 7th edition. (New York: Thomson and Heinle, 2003).
A readable general introduction, helped along by cartoons and quotations.

Hudson, G. *Essential introductory linguistics*. (Oxford: Blackwell, 2000).
A clear and straightforward guide.

O'Grady, W., Dobrovolsky, M. and Katamba, F. *Contemporary linguistics: An introduction*. (London: Addison Wesley Longman, 1997).
A clear introduction, with a good chapter on syntax.

Pinker, S. *The language instinct: The new science of language and mind*. (London: Allen Lane, The Penguin Press, 1994).
A wide ranging overview within a biological framework.

Radford, A., Atkinson, M., Britain, D., Clahsen, H. and Spencer A. *Linguistics: An introduction*. (Cambridge: Cambridge University Press, 1999).
A straightforward, no-nonsense textbook.

Wardaugh, R. *Understanding English grammar: A linguistic approach*, 2nd edition. (Oxford: Blackwell, 2003).
A clear and accessible account.

Weisler, S.E. and Milekic, S. *Theory of language*. (Cambridge, MA: MIT Press, 2000).
Clearly written, but dives fast into some quite complex issues.

Yule, G. *The study of language*, 2nd edition. (Cambridge: Cambridge University Press, 1996).
A broad-ranging outline survey.

Books of readings, dictionaries and encyclopaedias

Clark, V.P., Escholz, P.A. and Rosa, A.F. (eds.) *Language: introductory readings*, 5th edition. (New York: St. Martin's Press, 1997).
A range of readable readings on different topics within linguistics.

Crystal, D. *A dictionary of linguistics and phonetics*, 5th edition. (Oxford: Blackwell, 2002).
Useful guide to terminology.

Crystal, D. *The Cambridge encyclopaedia of language*, 2nd edition. (Cambridge: Cambridge University Press, 1997).
Intended for a general market, but informative and easy to read.

Crystal, D. *The Penguin dictionary of language*, 2nd edition. (London: Penguin, 1999).
A handy book covering both linguistic terms and major languages.

Fromkin, V. (ed.) *Linguistics: An introduction to linguistic theory*. (Oxford: Blackwell, 2000).
A 'gang of 12' from Los Angeles worked together on this clear textbook.

Malmkjaer, K. (ed.) *The linguistics encyclopaedia*, 2nd edition. (London: Routledge, 2002).
Over seventy substantial entries, covering most of linguistics, with references to further reading.

Matthews, P. *The concise Oxford dictionary of linguistics*. (Oxford: Oxford University Press, 1997)
A reliable guide.

Trask, L. *Key concepts in language and linguistics*. (London: Routledge, 1999).
A range of linguistic terms explained, with suggestions for further reading.

History of linguistics

Matthews, P. *Grammatical theory in the United States from Bloomfield to Chomsky*. (Cambridge: Cambridge University Press, 1993).
A useful book for understanding the concerns of 20th-century linguistics, though presumes some prior knowledge.

Robins, R.H. *A short history of linguistics*, 4th edition. (London: Longman, 1997).
A survey of linguistic ideas from ancient Greece to the present century.

Sound structure: phonetics and phonology

Clark, J. and Yallop, C. *An introduction to phonetics and phonology*, 2nd edition. (Oxford: Blackwell, 1995).
A thorough account, better on phonetics than phonology.

Cruttenden, A. *Gimson's pronunciation of English*, 6th edition. (London: Arnold, 1994).
The standard guide to the sounds of British English.

Giegerich, H.J. *English phonology: An introduction*. (Cambridge: Cambridge University Press, 1992).
An account which covers both British and American English.

Goldsmith, J. (ed.) *The handbook of phonological theory.* (Oxford: Blackwell, 1994).
A fat tome, with essays by over thirty well-known phonologists on current issues.

Gussenhoven, C. and Jacobs, H. *Understanding phonology.* (London: Arnold, 1998).
A straightforward introduction.

Gussmann, E. *Phonology: Analysis and theory.* (Cambridge: Cambridge University Press, 2002).
A useful guide.

Hardcastle, W.J. and Laver, J. (eds.) *The handbook of phonetic sciences.* (Oxford: Blackwell, 1996).
A large, wide-ranging tome.

International Phonetics Association. *Handbook of the International Phonetics Association.* (Cambridge: Cambridge University Press, 1999).
A phonetic description of the IPA, with illustrations from twenty-nine different languages.

Kager, R. *Optimality theory.* (Cambridge: Cambridge University Press, 1999).
An introduction to this trendy topic, which is important for phonology.

Ladefoged, P. *A course in phonetics*, 4th edition (New York: Harcourt, 2001).
A broad general introduction, covering sounds from a wide variety of languages.

Ladefoged, P. and Maddieson, I. *The sounds of the world's languages.* (Oxford: Blackwell, 1996).
A survey of the sounds made by the languages of the world.

Laver, J. *Principles of phonetics.* (Cambridge: Cambridge University Press, 1994).
A useful overview.

Pullum, G. and Ladusaw, W.A. *Phonetic symbol guide*, 2nd edition. (Chicago: Chicago University Press, 1996).
A comprehensive survey of the phonetic symbols used in linguistics texts.

Roach, P. *English phonetics and phonology: A practical course*, 3rd edition. (Cambridge: Cambridge University Press, 2000).
A clear account.

Roca, I. and Johnson, W. *A course in phonology.* (Oxford: Blackwell, 1999).
A clearly laid out course, which moves from the basic sounds, to stress and syllables, on to advanced ideas, including optimality theory.

Spencer, A. *Phonology*. (Oxford: Blackwell, 1996).
A no-nonsense introduction.

Wells, J.C. *Accents of English*, vol.1–3. (Cambridge:
Cambridge University Press, 1982).
A survey of the various types of English accent found both
in England and around the world.

Word structure: morphology

Bauer, L. *Introducing English morphology*. (Edinburgh:
Edinburgh University Press, 1988).
A lucid introduction to the study of word structure.

Spencer, A. *Morphological theory*. (Oxford: Blackwell, 1991).
An overview of current morphological theory.

Spencer, A. and Zwicky, A.M. (eds.) *The handbook of
morphology*. (Oxford: Blackwell, 1997).
A fat tome with both traditional topics and newer areas.

Sentence structure: syntax – general

Börjars, K. and Burridge, K. *Introducing English grammar*.
(London: Arnold, 2001).
An introduction with clear explanations and amusing
examples.

Borsley, R.D. *Syntactic theory: A unified approach*, 2nd
edition. (London: Edward Arnold, 1999).
An attempt to show how different schools of thought within
linguistics have handled important areas of syntax.

Lobeck, A. *Discovering grammar: An introduction to English
sentence structure*. (Oxford: Oxford University Press, 2000).
A clear, no-nonsense introduction, with good diagrams of
sentence structure.

Morenberg, M. *Doing grammar*. (Oxford: Oxford University
Press, 1991).
A lucid beginning book.

Palmer, F. *Grammatical roles and relations*. (Cambridge:
Cambridge University Press, 1994).
An outline account of roles such as agent, patient, and
relations such as subject, object.

Quirk, R., Greenbaum, S., Leech, G. and Svartvik, J. *A
comprehensive grammar of the English language* (London:
Longman, 1985).
A mammoth reference book, usable without any knowledge
of linguistics.

Thomas, L. *Beginning syntax*. (Oxford: Blackwell, 1993).
An informative, step-by-step guide.

Meaning: semantics

Chierchia, G. and McConnell-Ginet, S. *Meaning and grammar* (Cambridge, MA: MIT Press, 1990).

A reliable but fairly technical introduction to semantics.

Frawley, W. *Linguistic semantics.* (Hillsdale, NJ: Lawrence Erlbaum, 1992).

Tries to relate semantics to the 'real world'.

Goddard, C. *Semantic analysis: A practical introduction.* (Oxford: Oxford University Press, 1998).

A wide-ranging introduction which includes cultural issues.

Lappin, S. (ed.) *The handbook of contemporary semantic theory.* (Oxford: Blackwell, 1996).

A fat tome which deals with most current areas of semantic enquiry – though not for beginners.

Lyons, J. *Linguistic semantics: An introduction.* (Cambridge: Cambridge University Press, 1995).

A sane discussion of various important issues, though not always easy for beginners.

Saeed, J.I. *Semantics.* (Oxford: Blackwell, 1997).

A down-to-earth textbook covering the main areas of semantics.

Taylor, J.R. *Linguistic categorization: Prototypes in linguistic theory*, 2nd edition. (Oxford: Clarendon Press, 1995).

A clear account of prototype theory.

Ungerer, F. and Schmid, H.-J. *An introduction to cognitive linguistics.* (London: Longman, 1996).

A book which bridges the gap between semantics and psycholinguistics.

Language use: pragmatics

Aijmer, K. *Conversational routines in English: Convention and creativity.* (London: Longman, 1996).

Thanking, requesting, apologizing, and offering in English.

Davis, S. (ed.) *Pragmatics: A reader.* (Oxford: Oxford University Press, 1991).

A useful collection of readings, including some 'classics'.

Grundy, P. *Doing pragmatics.* (London: Arnold, 1995).

A user-friendly overview.

Mey, J. *Pragmatics: An introduction.* (Oxford: Blackwell, 1993).

A book which concentrates on a speech act approach.

Schiffrin, D. *Approaches to discourse.* (Oxford: Blackwell, 1993).

Explains and compares different approaches to analyzing discourse.

Schiffrin, D., Tannen, D. and Hamilton, H.E. *The handbook of discourse analysis.* (Oxford: Blackwell, 2001).
A wide-ranging tome with more than forty papers.

Tannen, D. *That's not what I meant!: How conversational style makes or breaks your relations with others.* (London: Virago, 1992).
A popularizing book, useful as an introduction to conversational analysis.

Language and society: sociolinguistics

Chambers, J.K. *Sociolinguistic theory.* (Oxford: Blackwell, 1995).
A broad-ranging survey of language variation, including its biological significance.

Chambers, J.K., Trudgill, P. and Schilling-Estes, N. *The handbook of language variation and change.* (Oxford: Blackwell, 2002).
A fat volume, with twenty-nine papers on various aspects of variation.

Cheshire, J. and Trudgill, P. (eds.) *The sociolinguistics reader, (vol.2): Gender and discourse.* (London: Arnold, 1998).
A useful collection of papers; see also Trudgill and Cheshire (vol.1).

Coates, J. *Women, men and language,* 2nd edition. (London: Longman, 1993).
A clear account of research on language and gender.

Downes, W. *Language and society,* 2nd edition. (Cambridge: Cambridge University Press, 1998).
An overview which links sociolinguistics and pragmatics.

Eckert, P. and McConnell-Ginet, S. *Language and gender.* (Cambridge: Cambridge University Press, 2002).
Assesses the relationship between gender and language use.

Holmes, J. *An introduction to sociolinguistics,* 2nd edition. (London: Longman, 2001).
A clear account, divided into multilingualism, user variation, and use variation.

Holmes, J. *Women, men and politeness.* (London: Longman, 1995).
How men and women differ in their use of verbal politeness.

Montgomery, M. *An introduction to language and society,* 2nd edition. (London: Routledge, 1995).
Broad coverage which includes the role of language in shaping social relationships.

Romaine, S. *Language in society: An introduction to sociolinguistics*, 2nd edition. (Oxford: Oxford University Press, 2000).
Brief and sensible.
Todd, L. *Modern Englishes: Pidgins and creoles*, 2nd edition. (London: Routledge, 1990).
An introductory survey.
Trudgill, P. *Sociolinguistics*, 4th edition. (London: Penguin, 2000).
Clear, brief and interesting account of language variation.
Trudgill, P. and Cheshire, J. *The sociolinguistics reader, vol.1: Multilingualism and variation.* (London: Arnold, 1998).
A useful collection of readings, see also Cheshire and Trudgill (vol.2).
Wardaugh, R. *An introduction to sociolinguistics*, 3rd edition. (Oxford: Blackwell, 1998).
A wide-ranging outline survey.

Language and mind: psycholinguistics

Aitchison, J. *The articulate mammal: An introduction to psycholinguistics*, 4th edition. (London: Routledge, 1998).
A readable introduction to the acquisition, comprehension and production of speech.
Aitchison, J. *Words in the mind: An introduction to the mental lexicon*, 3rd edition. (Oxford: Blackwell, 2002).
A user-friendly account of how people learn, store and retrieve words.
Altmann, G.T.M. *The ascent of Babel: An exploration of language, mind and understanding.* (Oxford: Oxford University Press, 1997).
An introduction to language from the point of view of a psychologist.
Berko-Gleason, J. (ed.) *The development of language*, 3rd edition. (New York: Charles Merrill, 1993).
A useful survey anthology, fairly easy to read.
Berko-Gleason, J. and Ratner, N.B. (eds.) *Psycholinguistics*, 2nd edition. (New York: Harcourt-Brace, 1998).
Another useful survey anthology.
Bloom, P. (ed.) *Language acquisition: Core readings.* (Cambridge, MA: MIT Press, 1994).
A book of readings which tries to balance theory and description.

Chiat, S. *Understanding children with language problems.* (Cambridge: Cambridge University Press, 2000). A survey of things that can go wrong with children's language.

Fletcher, P. and Garman, M. (eds.) *The handbook of child language.* (Oxford: Blackwell, 1994). Essays written by twenty-five specialists on current issues.

Miller, J.L. and Eimas, P.D. (eds.) *Speech, language and comprehension.* (London: Academic Press, 1995). An overview by well-known researchers.

Obler, L.K. and Gjerlow, K. *Language and the brain.* (Cambridge: Cambridge University Press, 1999). A concise and accessible book on language in the brain both in normal people and brain-damaged patients.

Language and style: stylistics

Bell, A. *The language of news media.* (Oxford: Blackwell, 1991). A clear introduction from an ex-journalist who is now an academic.

Cook, G. *The discourse of advertising*, 2nd edition. (London: Routledge, 2001). The language of contemporary advertising, including its links to literary language.

Fabb, N. *Linguistics and literature.* (Oxford: Blackwell, 1997). Relates linguistic theory to literature around the world.

Freeborn, D. *Style: Text analysis and linguistic criticism.* (London: Macmillan, 1996). A wide-ranging book which includes traditional rhetoric and news reporting.

Myers, G. *Ad worlds: Brands, media, audiences.* (London: Arnold, 1999). An accessible introduction which looks both at the ads, and the audiences they are aiming at.

Short, M. *Exploring the language of poems, plays and prose.* (London: Longman, 1996). As its title suggests, it concentrates on prose, plays and verse.

Tanaka, K. *Advertising language: A pragmatic approach to advertisements in Britain and Japan.* (London: Routledge, 1994). A comparison of advertisements in two different cultures.

Toolan, M. *Language in literature: An introduction to stylistics.* (London: Arnold, 1998). A range of topics are discussed.

Wales, K. *A dictionary of stylistics* (London: Longman, 1989).
A useful dictionary of widely-used terms.
Weber, J.J. *The stylistics reader: From Roman Jakobson to the present*. (London: Arnold, 1996).
A well-chosen set of readings.

Language change: historical linguistics

Aitchison, J. *Language change: progress or decay?*, 3rd edition. (Cambridge: Cambridge University Press, 2001).
A readable survey of basic issues in language change, including links with social variation.
Barber, C. *The English language: A historical introduction*. (Cambridge: Cambridge University Press, 1993).
An easy-to-read survey.
Beekes, R.S.P. *Comparative Indo-European linguistics: An introduction*. (Amsterdam: John Benjamins, 1995).
The title summarizes its content.
Campbell, L. *Historical linguistics*. (Edinburgh: Edinburgh University Press, 1998).
A useful overview, with examples from a wide range of languages, including American-Indian ones.
Crowley, T. *An introduction to historical linguistics*, 3rd edition. (Oxford: Oxford University Press, 1997).
Good on linguistic reconstruction with useful examples from Polynesian languages.
Fox, A. *Linguistic reconstruction: An introduction to theory and method*. (Oxford: Oxford University Press, 1995).
A useful overview of the various methods.
McMahon, A. *Understanding language change*. (Cambridge: Cambridge University Press, 1994).
A clear textbook for those who have already had an introduction to the subject.

Language typology and language universals

Comrie, B. *Language universals and linguistic typology*, 2nd edn. (Oxford: Blackwell, 1989).
A clear survey of attempts to divide languages up into different types.
Croft, W. *Typology and universals*, 2nd edition. (Cambridge: Cambridge University Press, 2002).
An overview of typology which stresses the role of functional and historical explanations.

Song, J.J. *Linguistic typology*. (London: Longman, 2001).
A work which focuses on major syntactic patterns.

The world's languages

Comrie, B. (ed.) *The world's major languages*, updated edition.
(London: Croom Helm/Routledge, 1987).
A useful survey, each chapter provided by an expert in the
area.

Comrie, B., Matthews, S. and Polinsky, M. *The atlas of
languages*. (London: Bloomsbury, 1997).
Clear maps show the location of the world's main
languages.

Ruhlen, M. *A guide to the world's languages, vol.1:
Classification*. (Stanford, CA: Stanford University Press,
1987).
An extensive list of all known languages, with information
about their genetic classification.

Attitudes to language

Bailey, R.W. *Images of English: A cultural history of the
language*. (Cambridge: Cambridge University Press, 1992).
A history of ideas about the English language.

Bex, T. and Watts, R.J. (eds.) *Standard English: The widening
debate*. (London: Routledge, 1999).
Explores the standard language question from a variety of
angles.

Cameron, D. *Verbal hygiene*. (London: Routledge, 1995).
Popular attitudes towards language, especially the notion
that it should be 'cleaned up'.

Milroy, J. and Milroy, L. *Authority in language: Investigating
language prescription and standardization*, 2nd edition.
(London: Routledge, 1991).
An overview of the 'complaint tradition'.

Mugglestone, L. *Talking proper: The rise of accent as a social
symbol*. (Oxford: Clarendon Press, 1995).
A well-documented survey.

Corpus linguistics and computational analysis

Barnbrook, G. *Language and computers: A practical
introduction to the computer analysis of language*.
(Edinburgh: Edinburgh University Press, 1996).
A wide-ranging overview.

Biber, D., Conrad, S. and Reppen, R. *Corpus linguistics: Investigating language structure and use.* (Cambridge: Cambridge University Press, 1998).
Shows the wide range of applications: each chapter is devoted to a different area within linguistics.

Kennedy, G. *An introduction to corpus linguistics.* (London: Longman, 1998).
An overview which surveys major work already done.

Meyer, C.F. *English corpus linguistics: An introduction.* (Cambridge: Cambridge University Press, 2002).
Practical information on how to create a corpus.

Chomsky's approach

Chomsky, N. edited by Belletti A. and Rizzi, L. *On nature and language,* (Cambridge: Cambridge University Press, 2002).
Chomsky's own recent views, including an outline of the Minimalist Program.

Cook, V.J. and Newson, M. *Chomsky's universal grammar: An introduction,* 2nd edition. (Oxford: Blackwell, 1996).
An outline account of Chomsky's work in the 1980s and 1990s.

Maher, J. and Groves, J. *Chomsky for beginners.* (Cambridge: Icon Books, 1996).
Easy reading, with lots of pictures.

Ouhalla, J. *Introducing transformational grammar: From rules to principles and parameters.* (London: Arnold, 1994).
A straightforward, useful course.

Radford, A. *Syntax: A minimalist introduction.* (Cambridge: Cambridge University Press, 1997).
An abridged version of a longer, simultaneously published book by the same author on Chomsky's Minimalist Program.

list of symbols and abbreviations

(Phonetic symbols used are listed on pp. 46–7 and pp. 244 ff.)

[ ]	used for phonetic transcription
/ /	used for phonemic transcription
( )	denotes an optional item
$\begin{Bmatrix} X \\ Y \end{Bmatrix}$	indicates alternatives, 'either X or Y'
*	indicates an ill-formed sentence or word
!	indicates a semantically impossible sentence
→	means 'rewrite as'
ø	means 'zero'
#	indicates a word boundary
/	means 'in the environment of'
	e.g. [l] → [ɬ] – means rewrite [l] as [ɬ]
	before a word boundary (i.e. at the end of a word)
S	Sentence
N	Noun
NP	Noun phrase
V	Verb
VP	Verb phrase
A	Adjective
AP	Adjective phrase
P	Preposition
PP	Preposition phrase

Speech sounds may be described and classified mainly in two ways:

- in **articulatory** terms (means of production)
- in **acoustic** terms (analysis of sound waves).

The following brief descriptions are all **articulatory**.

Consonants and vowels

The traditional distinction between consonantal-type sounds and vowel-type sounds is a useful one (though closer analysis shows that it is not as clear-cut or as easy to define as appears at first sight).

English consonants

English consonantal sounds are those which are most easily described in terms of three variables:

- voicing
- place of articulation
- manner of articulation.

Voicing

The vocal cords are thin strips of membrane in the throat (see Figure 1). If they vibrate as a sound is produced, it is said to be **voiced**, as in the production of [b d g v ð z ʒ dʒ m n ŋ l r w j]. This vibration can be felt if a hand is placed on the outside of the throat as the sound is uttered. If the vocal cords do not vibrate as a sound is produced, it is said to be **voiceless**, as in [p t k f θ s ʃ tʃ].

Place of articulation

The **place of articulation** describes the point at which the articulators actually touch, or are at their closest. The most important places for the production of English sounds are listed in the table below. See also Figure 1.

	Articulators	**Examples**
BILABIAL	Upper lip + lower lip	[p b m]
DENTAL	Teeth + tongue	[θ ð]
LABIO-DENTAL	Lower lip + upper teeth	[f v]
ALVEOLAR	Alveolar (teeth) ridge + tongue	[t d s z r l n]
PALATO-ALVEOLAR	Join of hard palate and alveolar ridge + tongue	[ʃ ʒ tʃ dʒ]
PALATAL	Hard palate + tongue	[j]
VELAR	Soft palate + tongue	[k g]
GLOTTAL	Vocal cords	[h ʔ]

Table 1

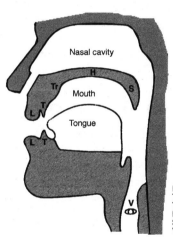

L. Lips
T. Teeth
Tr. Teeth ridge
H. Hard palate
S. Soft palate
V. Vocal cords

figure 1

Manner of articulation

The **manner of articulation** describes the type of obstruction caused by the narrowing or closure of the articulators.

	Movement of articulators	Examples
STOP (PLOSIVE)	Complete closure	[p b t d k g]
AFFRICATE	Closure, then slow separation	[tʃ dʒ]
FRICATIVE	Narrowing, resulting in audible friction	[f v θ ð s z]
NASAL	Complete closure in mouth, air escapes through nose	[m n ŋ]
LATERAL	Closure in centre of mouth, air escapes down sides	[l]
APPROXIMANT	Slight narrowing, not enough to cause friction	[w j r]

Table 2

Identification of sounds

Any English sound can be described and identified in the above terms:

e.g. [s] is a **voiceless alveolar fricative**
[b] is a **voiced bilabial stop**
[tʃ] is a **voiceless palato-alveolar affricate**.

This information can also be conveniently plotted on a chart (Table 3, opposite).

Note that w occurs twice, as a velar, and also (in brackets) as a labial. This is because it is technically a **labial-velar approximant**, with a double place of articulation.

The account opposite is by no means a complete phonetic description. It represents the minimum necessary for distinguishing between English consonantal-type phonemes in articulatory terms. Note also that there are sometimes minor variations and disagreements as to how to describe a particular sound.

		BILABIAL	LABIO DENTAL	DENTAL	ALVEOLAR	PALATO-ALVEOLAR	PALATAL	VELAR	GLOTTAL
STOP	vless	p			t			k	ʔ
	vd	b			d			g	
AFFRICATE	vless					tʃ			
	vd					dʒ			
FRICATIVE	vless		f	θ	s	ʃ			h
	vd		v	ð	z	ʒ			
NASAL	m	m		n				ŋ	
LATERAL				l					
APPROXIMANT		(w)			r		j	w	

Table 3

Notes

Other common phonetic terms and symbols sometimes used to describe consonants are:

1. **Sibilant.** A general term used to denote 'hissing' and 'hushing' sounds, e.g. [s z ʃ ʒ].
2. **Liquid.** A general term used to cover [l] and [r].
3. **Semi-vowel.** A general term used to cover [j] and [w].
4. **Frictionless continuant.** An older term for what is now usually called an **approximant**.
5. **Syllabic nasals** [m̩] [n̩]. Nasal consonants which constitute a whole syllable, as in some pronunciations of *madam* [mædm̩], *garden* [gɑːdn̩]. Liquids can also be syllabic, as in *funnel* [fʌnl̩] and American English *ladder* [lædɹ̩].

English vowels

Vowel-type sounds are those in which the sound depends mainly on variations in the position of the tongue. They are normally voiced. English vowel-type sounds are most easily described in terms of two variables.

*   **height of the tongue**
*   **part of the tongue** which is raised or lowered.

In the description of vowels, **lip-rounding** is usually added as a third variable. But in British English, front and central vowels are automatically unrounded, and back vowels (except [ɑː]) are automatically rounded. So this distinction has been omitted. Note, however, that in describing French and German vowels, lip-rounding is a major variable.

Vowels are normally plotted onto a diagram which represents the possible limits of human vowels. This diagram is constituted by setting up four extreme points (Figures 2–3).

In Figure 2, the following extremes are illustrated.

[i] shows the tongue at its highest and farthest forward
[a] shows the tongue at its lowest and farthest forward
[u] shows the tongue at its highest and farthest back
[ɑ] shows the tongue at its lowest and farthest back.

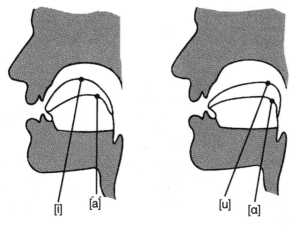

figure 2

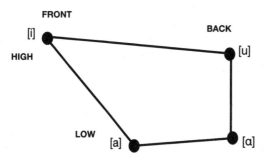

figure 3

Between these extreme four points, [e] and [ɛ] are marked equidistant between [i] and [a], and [o] and [ɔ] are marked equidistant between [u] and [ɑ].

These eight points were called the **cardinal vowels** by Daniel Jones, who devised this system, and the vowels of any language can be plotted onto this quadrilateral (Figure 4, p. 250).

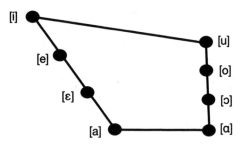

figure 4

English vowel sounds are of two types:

- relatively **pure**, or unchanging vowels, as in *set, sat, sit*
- **diphthongs**, or gliding vowels, as in *boat, bite, boil* in which the tongue position alters as the sound is made.

The **pure vowels** are fairly easy to plot on the cardinal vowel diagram (though the placing is only approximate owing to the large amount of variation found in British vowel sounds). Two dots beside a vowel indicate **length**, e.g. [uː]

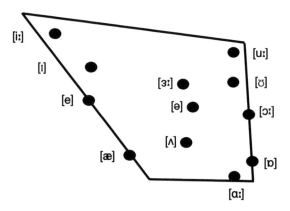

figure 5

A less accurate, but useful schematic diagram, is as follows

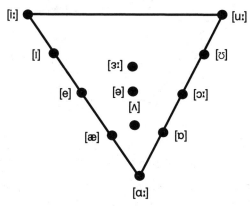

figure 6

Diphthongs are shown by arrows linking the tongue positions:

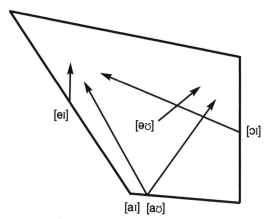

figure 7

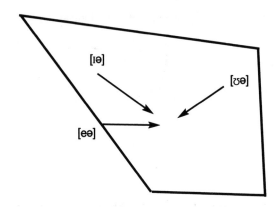

figure 8

teach yourself ®

Hinduism
History, 101 Key Ideas
How to Win at Horse Racing
How to Win at Poker
HTML Publishing on the WWW
Human Anatomy & Physiology
Hungarian
Icelandic
Indian Head Massage
Indonesian
Information Technology, 101 Key Ideas
Internet, The
Irish
Islam
Italian
Italian, Beginner's
Italian Grammar
Italian Grammar, Quick Fix
Italian, Instant
Italian, Improve your
Italian Language, Life & Culture
Italian Verbs
Italian Vocabulary
Japanese
Japanese, Beginner's
Japanese, Instant
Japanese Language, Life & Culture
Japanese Script, Beginner's
Java
Jewellery Making
Judaism
Korean
Latin
Latin American Spanish
Latin, Beginner's
Latin Dictionary
Latin Grammar
Letter Writing Skills
Linguistics
Linguistics, 101 Key Ideas
Literature, 101 Key Ideas
Mahjong
Managing Stress
Marketing
Massage
Mathematics
Mathematics, Basic
Media Studies
Meditation
Mosaics
Music Theory
Needlecraft
Negotiating
Nepali

Norwegian
Origami
Panjabi
Persian, Modern
Philosophy
Philosophy of Mind
Philosophy of Religion
Philosophy of Science
Philosophy, 101 Key Ideas
Photography
Photoshop
Physics
Piano
Planets
Planning Your Wedding
Polish
Politics
Portuguese
Portuguese, Beginner's
Portuguese Grammar
Portuguese, Instant
Portuguese Language, Life & Culture
Postmodernism
Pottery
Powerpoint 2002
Presenting for Professionals
Project Management
Psychology
Psychology, 101 Key Ideas
Psychology, Applied
Quark Xpress
Quilting
Recruitment
Reflexology
Reiki
Relaxation
Retaining Staff
Romanian
Russian
Russian, Beginner's
Russian Grammar
Russian, Instant
Russian Language, Life & Culture
Russian Script, Beginner's
Sanskrit
Screenwriting
Serbian
Setting up a Small Business
Shorthand, Pitman 2000
Sikhism
Spanish
Spanish, Beginner's
Spanish Grammar
Spanish Grammar, Quick Fix

Spanish, Instant
Spanish, Improve your
Spanish Language, Life & Culture
Spanish Starter Kit
Spanish Verbs
Spanish Vocabulary
Speaking on Special Occasions
Speed Reading
Statistical Research
Statistics
Swahili
Swahili Dictionary
Swedish
Tagalog
Tai Chi
Tantric Sex
Teaching English as a Foreign Language
Teaching English One to One
Teams and Team-Working
Thai
Time Management
Tracing your Family History
Travel Writing
Trigonometry
Turkish
Turkish, Beginner's
Typing
Ukrainian
Urdu
Urdu Script, Beginner's
Vietnamese
Volcanoes
Watercolour Painting
Weight Control through Diet and
  Exercise
Welsh
Welsh Dictionary
Welsh Language, Life & Culture
Wills and Probate
Wine Tasting
Winning at Job Interviews
Word 2002
World Faiths
Writing a Novel
Writing for Children
Writing Poetry
Xhosa
Yoga
Zen
Zulu

available from bookshops and on-line retailers